GIVING MEANINGS
TO THE WORLD

Recent Titles in
Contributions to the Study of Mass Media and Communications

GIVING MEANINGS TO THE WORLD

The First U.S. Foreign Correspondents,
1838–1859

GIOVANNA DELL'ORTO

Contributions to the Study of Mass Media and Communications, Number 64

GREENWOOD PRESS
Westport, Connecticut • London

Library of Congress Cataloging-in-Publication Data

Dell'Orto, Giovanna, 1977—
    Giving meanings to the world : the first U.S. foreign correspondents,
    1838–1859 / Giovanna Dell'Orto.
        p.   cm.—(Contributions to the study of mass media and communications,
    ISSN 0732–4456 ; no. 64)
    Includes bibliographical references.
    ISBN 0–313–32290–2 (alk. paper)
    1. Foreign news—United States—History—19th century. 2. Foreign
correspondents—United States—Biography. I. Title. II. Series.
PN4888.F69D45   2002
070.4′332′097309034—dc21   2001058636

British Library Cataloguing in Publication Data is available.

Library of Congress Catalog Card Number: 2001058636
ISBN: 0–313–32290–2
ISSN: 0732–4456

First published in 2002

Greenwood Press, 88 Post Road West, Westport, CT 06881
An imprint of Greenwood Publishing Group, Inc.
www.greenwood.com

Printed in the United States of America

The paper used in this book complies with the
Permanent Paper Standard issued by the National
Information Standards Organization (Z39.48–1984).

10 9 8 7 6 5 4 3 2 1

Copyright Acknowledgments

The author and the publisher gratefully acknowledge permission for use of the following material:

Extracts from Lou Boccardi, "Introduction," in Otto C. Doelling, ed. *Handbook for
International Correspondents* (The Associated Press, 1998). Reprinted with permission from Lou Boccardi, President and CEO of The Associated Press.

Contents

PREFACE

In 1859, the editor of the *New York Times* admonished fellow U.S. editors not to rely for their international coverage on the words of "a single electrician at a seaport town," by which he meant the reporting by foreign newspapers transmitted over the Atlantic via telegraph operators.

Twenty years earlier, editors relied upon the foreign newspaper reports for all of their international coverage. Beginning in 1838, however, while the "electricians" and their pre-telegraph predecessors kept compiling terse news digests, the real foreign news came from an increasingly large corps of foreign correspondents roaming the world to give a firsthand report to the American public. Often patriotic, sometimes subtly controversial, always witty, informative, and analytical, the earliest U.S. foreign correspondence helped to give meanings to foreign cultures and to instill them in the American consciousness at the crucial moment when the nation transformed itself from an experiment in democracy into a world power.

What kind of image of France was created for the cattle businessman who read the newspaper in St. Louis? What type of image of Japan was given to the New York women's rights activist reading one of the metropolis' dailies? This book explores the images of foreign countries that emerge from the first formally organized American foreign correspondence, focusing on the discourse of the "world" constructed in mid-nineteenth-century correspondence.

By emphasizing the emergence of foreign correspondence across its first two decades, both in mainstream and "alternative" outlets, and comparing the ways it constructed the "world" with images in editorials and in congressional debates of the time, the book addresses the pivotal question of what meanings were given to foreign cultures by the first U.S. foreign correspondents. In general, this question has been largely unasked by the literature on foreign correspondents and journalism history. While the literature tends to focus on how well (usually how badly) "great" correspondents have covered world events, the book focuses on how the earliest, often anonymous correspondents helped shape an American common sense about the rest of the world.

The birth of U.S. foreign correspondence coincided with the popularization of newspapers and the professionalization of journalists. Most importantly, the correspondence constructed the world for an America that believed like never before, or, arguably, after, in its providential, superior position, destined to lead the rest of the world to enlightenment by example and intervention.

Most of the correspondents constructed meanings that helped maintain this common sense about foreign cultures. Even correspondents for an African American newspaper and women writers did not question the United States' role in the world other than by arguing that the country should better itself before being able to fulfill its superior destiny.

Some correspondents for mainstream newspapers, however, did challenge, though ambivalently, such constructions; apparently, an increased familiarity with the countries they covered made them uneasy with assigning understandings to foreign cultures that were based more on unfavorable comparisons with America than on the other countries' own faults and merits.

While the book does not seek to draw comparisons with current U.S. foreign correspondence, some of the concerns that the earliest correspondents had and some of their images and, often, prejudices—their discourses of the "world"—will strongly resonate with modern-day media consumers and journalists. That some of the earliest correspondents managed to challenge dominant discourses of the "world" will, it is hoped, encourage today's journalists abroad to do the same as well as spur newspaper business people to keep a substantial corps of reporters abroad to challenge and complicate the American discourse of the world.

ACKNOWLEDGMENTS

Before concluding this brief introduction, a caveat and acknowledgments are in order. Lengthy quotations from mid-nineteenth-century correspondence are used in this text to illustrate the various constructions of the "world," as well as to enable readers to familiarize themselves with the style and idiosyncrasies of the correspondents and to preserve historical accuracy. The views of the "world" and particular countries or peoples, however, that transpire from those writings, often in strong language, should not in any sense be read as representative of the views of the author, editor, or publisher.

Finally, it is quite impossible to enumerate all the many people whose professional and personal support was crucial to this project. It is, however, a much easier task to know how to begin such a list—by expressing my sincere gratitude to Dr. Hazel Dicken-Garcia at the University of Minnesota School of Journalism and Mass Communication. For many years, working with her has been both a pleasure and a spur to continuous intellectual and personal growth. The significance of her painstaking scholarship, her committed professionalism, and her generous mentorship for my development as a person, let alone as a scholar, cannot be overestimated.

I am also especially grateful to University of Minnesota Drs. Nancy Roberts, School of Journalism and Mass Communication, and Frederick Asher, Department of Art History, for their suggestions and for challenging and fostering my understanding of cultures in the realms of literature and art. My special appreciation goes to Dr. Albert Tims, director of the University of Minnesota School of Journalism and Mass Communication. I am grateful for the trust and the encouragement the school has shown me throughout the years, by generous support and a constant quest for ways to enrich my academic career. Under Dr. Tims' leadership, Murphy Hall is a place that I am proud to call my alma mater. Of course, such a thriving milieu would not exist without the collegiality and scholarship of the school's faculty and staff, who also have my deep gratitude, especially Drs. Don Gillmor, Bill Babcock, Ken Doyle, and Kathleen Hansen; Joel Kramer, Senior Fellow; Linda Lindholm and Lisa Higgs in administration.

For suggestions and criticism, my thanks also to Dr. Kinley Brauer, University of Minnesota; Dr. David Sachsman, University of Tennessee at Chattanooga; Dr. Lauren Kessler, University of Oregon; Dr. Clint C. Wilson, Howard University; and the anonymous reviewers of this manuscript. It has been a pleasure to work with my editors, Eric Levy and Athan Metsopoulos II.

In the research for this book, I have relied perhaps most of all on the unfailing courtesy and efficiency of staffs at the University of Minnesota's Sevareid Library (especially Jan Nyberg) and Wilson Library; there, I extend my gratitude particularly to Becky Hoffman and the rest of the Interlibrary Loan office, to reference librarian Karen Beavers, and to the staff of the annex collection. They all have my thanks for the graciousness and skill with which they accommodated my elusive requests and endless renewals.

For giving me a firsthand appreciation of the intricacies of foreign reporting for American media, the staff of The Associated Press deserves mention; my thanks to AP colleagues in New York (especially President Louis Boccardi), Minneapolis, Rome, and particularly Phoenix. Under the direction of Steve Elliott and Eduardo Montes, the AP Arizona staff has been an excellent laboratory to experience how reporters handle international news on the always-controversial U.S.-Mexico border.

Finally, I should thank my colleagues and friends; they have kept challenging me and cheering me on, even though I fear my acknowledgment of their crucial support thus far has mostly been expressed as, "Sorry, I can't talk now, I have to finish my book."

It goes without saying that none of the above, or what follows, would exist if it hadn't been for my parents' unwavering support. Quite simply, to my father and mother, Dario and Paola Dell'Orto, I owe all. For my debt to them, words come woefully short. I can only hope this work—dedicated to them—can make them proud of how they have helped open my eyes to the world.

CHAPTER 1

EXPANDING MEANINGS OF THE "WORLD"

Amidst the Civil War, a Southern newspaper editor printed on the front page a lengthy article from a correspondent in Italy about the inauguration of the "monumental cemetery" in Genoa[1]—anecdotal, but evidence nonetheless of U.S. journalists' continued interest in foreign news of all kinds. However, mass communication scholars have largely ignored the realm of foreign correspondence, especially in its early developments in the nineteenth century. As will be discussed in this chapter, journalism scholars and professionals who have directed attention to foreign news have been concerned with biographies of "great" correspondents. Interest in foreign news—cast as international communications—has been almost exclusively in a twentieth-century, post-colonialist, center-periphery world-order frame focused on flow of news. And historians of the field have left nearly unexplored the evolution of foreign correspondence and the role of the foreign correspondent during the nineteenth century.

Who the early correspondents were; how they helped define their occupation, ethics, and conduct; what they reported on; what standards and expectations they created for foreign correspondence from the end of the colonial period to the time the United States became established as a world power—all these questions have yet to be fully addressed. Differing, however, from the vast majority of research in international communication and journalism history itself, this book does not ask simply who reported what from where. Rather, adopting a ritual view of communication (as defined by James Carey, it focuses not on the transmission of information but on the representation of a society's shared beliefs),[2] the purpose of this book is to explore what "world" the first American foreign correspondents "constructed" in their writings.

The purpose of this study is to identify the discourses in the earliest foreign correspondence from other nations to American newspapers, with the assumption that the earliest foreign correspondence helped shape a common sense for Americans about realities literally foreign to them. Of particular interest is the evolution of the representations of the "world" as constructed in the writings of foreign correspondents in American history. "World" is used here figuratively, not literally, for correspondents did not cover all parts of the world; rather, "world" stands here as a shorthand for anything foreign to the United States that the correspondents encountered abroad—foreign countries, peoples, customs, ideas—which constructed for readers some notion of the world. The focus is on the period between 1838–1860. Until 1838, foreign news was provided by digests reprinted from foreign newspapers. In 1838, James Gordon Bennett, editor of the *New York Herald*, sailed to Europe on the return trip of the first steamboat to cross the Atlantic with the purpose of establishing the first formal corps of foreign correspondents for an American newspaper. The *Herald* carried a letter from its London correspondent on July 17, 1838. By 1860, American journalism was on the eve of a revolution wrought by the Civil War; even more significantly for the history of foreign news, the Atlantic cable was successfully laid in 1866, allowing for much more rapid transmission of intercontinental news.

Beginning in 1838, for the first time, American newspaper readers were systematically offered views of foreign cultures through the eyes of fellow Americans living abroad and formally employed by newspapers as correspondents. Also in this period, the United States' political identity was being constructed as the nation evolved from an "experiment in democracy" to an established world power by the end of the nineteenth century.

Borrowing the idea from the theory of social construction of reality that meaning is not found but is socially created, this book seeks an answer to this overarching question: What meanings did the first U.S. correspondents give to foreign cultures through their reporting? Because of the paucity of secondary sources on foreign correspondence from 1838–1860, many areas of essential context were also researched—the prevalence of foreign news, the distinctiveness of correspondence compared to reprinted digests, the correspondents' perception of their occupation, and the images of the "world" in editorials and foreign policy discussions.

The way the "world" was represented in editorials and in congressional discussions is particularly relevant because, of all the filters correspondence went through—from sources in the foreign countries to editing in the home office—the contexts of how foreign realities were understood at the individual newspapers and generally in the domestic culture likely had the most influence. However, this book is not intended to investigate the different influences that might have shaped discourses; rather, the focus is on how foreign cultures were depicted, how those interpretations changed over time and whether alternative understandings existed, for example, in the writings of women correspondents. One reason that discourse is so powerful is that it operates at a subconscious level, so the historian might see the cultural implications of a text that would have appeared innocuously commonsensical to a contemporary reader. In fact, illuminating the construction of the common sense is one of the strengths and validations in studying discourse.

The political and social implications are evident—while this study does not seek to address directly the relationship between foreign correspondence and foreign policy, it is plausible that the evolution of a common understanding of foreign cultures influenced the evolution of U.S. foreign policies, and vice versa. Further, Daniel Goldhagen, in his study of anti-Semitism in Germany, has shown the powerfulness of the creation of a common sense about Jews through cognitive schemata in the writings of ordinary Germans preceding and during the Holocaust.[3] The immense consequences the creation of a common sense can have underscore the importance of a study of how foreign realities came to be constructed in the developing American nation.

Discursive content, though not assumed here to be necessarily in direct support of existing power structures, is defined as broadly ideological; that is, recurring discourse patterns represent prevailing summary, simplified, self-sustaining views of phenomena in a given society. Assuming that reality is brought into existence by communication through language and themes, we may be able to illuminate the process through which a meaning for foreign cultures was conveyed to American newspaper readers by a study of correspondents' writings. These findings from the very earliest foreign correspondence are crucial background to an understanding of how early American media have "constructed" the rest of the world for their readers. While comparisons with contemporary foreign correspondence would inevitably give way to unacceptable presentism and thus are not attempted here, knowledge of early understandings might foster understanding, and perhaps, with it, betterment of today's constructions of the "world."

It is impossible to show the effect constructions of the "world" might have had on the audience, or identify what a discourse meant to the readers, especially given the evolution of language since the nineteenth century; this study, though, can suggest a "common sense" identifiable in newspaper content and foreign policy records of a given period. For example, a *New York Herald* correspondent from Paris wrote in 1845: "Never did colony cost so dear and make so poor a return as Algeria has done to the French. To quell the *turbulent Arabs which surround and infest it*, the army there has been successively and continually augmented"[4] [italics added]. From the writer's words, it is evident that in his system of beliefs, Algeria's native population did not belong there, but amounted to an "infestation" of the country—a construction with obvious proto-imperialistic resonance. Thus, such texts both reflect and reinforce a particular discourse of the "other" (meant here as not American).

While not a central concern here, it should also be noted that constructions of the "other" construct, by default, the self. This means the correspondents, writing about foreign realities, were also implicitly defining themselves to some degree, especially their vision of the United States and of what it meant to be American.

This book, then, explores the constructions of foreign cultures discernible in selected American newspapers in the first two decades of formally organized foreign correspondence to those newspapers. Because of the paucity of secondary sources on foreign correspondence from 1838–1860, much information about essential context is missing. The question of the prevalence of foreign news from the 1830s to 1860 remains. Nor has there been a systematic study of the difference between the reprinted digests, eventually streamlined by The Associated Press, and correspondence by reporters abroad. Other than rare exceptions discussed in Chapter 2, little has been written about what the correspondents, often anonymous under their pen names and initials, thought about their role and the expectations for their new occupation. Finally, there has been no systematic study, for this period, of the press in relation to foreign policy. Therefore, some exploration of these areas was undertaken, although this was not the focus of research for the study.

The focus here, contrary to the overwhelming majority of foreign correspondence scholarship, is not on how well (usually how badly) foreign correspondents informed the American public of events occurring abroad—but on how they constructed the concept of "abroad" and a meaning for reality outside the United States.

Briefly, the concepts of social construction of reality and of discourse, described by Michel Foucault as a form of social knowledge,[5] embrace communication as creation and negotiation of meaning rather than as transmission of a fixed, presumed meaning. As Stuart Hall has argued, the question is not whether the news media objectively and fairly represent reality (in this case, whether the foreign correspondents objectively and fairly represented the world outside the United States); rather, the question is how written representations create a meaning for the realities that are reported.[6] Such an approach here goes beyond a study of the framing of foreign news, often emphasized in the context of propaganda and Third World coverage, to attempt to identify the discourses—the way other cultures were "talked about"—in the earliest foreign correspondence.

Theories on discourse are drawn from several disciplines, roughly divided into three groups: cultural, critical and literary theories; linguistics; and social psychology and critical linguistics.[7] The theory of social construction of reality was first proposed by Peter Berger and Thomas Luckmann in their 1966 book *The Social Construction of Reality*, whose pivotal tenet is relatively self-explanatory: "reality is socially constructed and [the] sociology of knowledge must analyze the processes in which this occurs." Thus, analysis of knowledge should focus on the means whereby "*any* body of 'knowledge' comes to be socially established *as* 'reality' "—which is the locus where other scholars see the constructive role of (media) discourse,[8] or the process which allows subjective meanings to become "objective facticities" and therefore creates an everyday world whose perceived reality is both engendered and maintained by human thought.[9] This process of knowledge revolves around "objectivations"; of these, a crucial case is signification (language), which both abstracts symbols from reality and also establishes them as real. Indeed, language is "both the basis and the instrument of the collective stock of knowledge."[10]

Berger and Luckmann introduced two other interrelated concepts of great consequence for the analysis of discourse: power and ideology. Power has a "socio-structural base" and determines whose definition of knowledge is acknowledged as reality; ideology is what this particular definition should be called when it is attached to an elite power interest.[11] Finally, such objectified reality is internalized as meaningful by the individual through socialization, which again can be the site of struggle and can indeed lead to a change in what definitions of reality are taken for granted in a certain society.[12]

There are three "layers" to discourse, according to Foucault: "The general domain of all statements," or discourse at the theoretical level; "an individualizable group of statements," or utterances that are somehow commonly bonded (for example, a discourse of imperialism or a discourse of the "world"); "a regulated practice that accounts for a number of statements," or the particular rules and structures that govern the production of text.[13] Throughout, one tenet of discourse remains pivotal—power, not only in its repressive quality but also in its insidious constructive capacity.

Power through discourse, however, does not mean that a common social knowledge is simply transferred from the dominating group to the powerless masses; rather, it is created in a struggle that makes questions of agency much less adamant.[14] This distinction is crucial to the perspective on discourse adopted in this study of foreign correspondence, where discursive constructions are not understood as imposed on the public by the press, which, in the first place, received them from a dominating elite; it is here deemed essential to understand discourse in a much broader, more fluid and interactive sense. In fact, discourse theory has been applied mostly to discourses of oppression, which are argued to have a powerful role in generally solidifying the disadvantaged position of society's historically least powerful groups, such as African Americans, women, and Third World people. Without denying that the very existence of a dominant discourse constitutes a form of social power, the perspective adopted here is aligned with the rarer examples of scholarship where discourse has been defined more broadly as the construction of a reality and its meaning, independent of immediate, coercive power structures.

Of those, perhaps the best example is Goldhagen's study of anti-Semitism in Nazi Germany. The author offers an explanation for the incredible willingness of ordinary Germans to become "Hitler's executioners" in the Holocaust that is rooted in a concept of anti-Semitism as German "common-sense." Goldhagen suggests that in fact Germans did not want to say "no" to the Holocaust because they believed that Jews ought to be eliminated—and this, because of the social construction of Jews, not only promoted by the Nazi powers, but intrinsic to German culture at the time.[15]

Even though Goldhagen does not specifically refer to his analysis as discourse, the entire book is based on the theoretical underpinnings of the creation of meaning. Indeed, he compares his inquiry to that of the anthropologist who explores "a radically different culture," seeking out its cognitive and value structures without assuming that they would appeal to his common sense. He suggests that an anti-Semitic view of the Jews as "fundamentally different and maleficent" had become self-evidently true to the Germans, a veritable part of their world order, and the Nazi regime only provided the opportunity for this cognitive schema to be activated.[16] In this hypothesis, Goldhagen offers a provoking problematization of discourse theory—he claims that uncovering cultural axioms of past societies is difficult because they are so commonplace that they might not be frequently articulated. In other words, Goldhagen is advising historical discourse analysts that the representations of discursive constructions might be most subtle when most culturally relevant.

Further, Goldhagen's research dramatically shows how terribly awry and disassociated from objective reality constructed meaning can be; he also suggests the power of "revolutionary" discourse—anti-Semitism was so ingrained in the German ethos that it managed to deny such dominant understandings as the value of human life, a tenet of Western civilization.[17] Goldhagen's analysis of an extraordinarily devastating example of the power of constructed reality warrants a reiteration of the concept of "common sense." As argued by Hall, "common sense" is the distillation of complex meanings, constructed by social knowledge and often provided by the press.[18] Goldhagen's study is instructive in showing not only the magnitude of the consequences of such discursive constructions, but also the capacity of such "common sense" to be created and widespread independently of time-specific elite interests.

Another example of creating a common sense, in this case for foreign realities, is in David Spurr's *The Rhetoric of Empire*, where he sought to identify and study the rhetorical features of colonial and postcolonial discourse and its usage since the last decades of the nineteenth century.[19] Even though this research purposely excludes the colonialist period in the attempt to identify a broader discourse in American press construction of foreign events, peoples, and cultures, Spurr's study remains significant because of its theoretical approach to the discourse of the "world" as well as the similarity between some of his findings and those discussed in this study.

Spurr defines colonial discourse as the collectivity of languages that both enabled and were generated by the process of colonization.[20] He identifies in colonial discourse a site and a stake in power struggles, often ridden with ambivalence as colonizers seek simultaneously to legitimize their position by establishing a radical difference from the subjects

and to justify the "morality" of colonization by insisting on a funda-
mental identity with the subjects.[21] He identifies a series of colonial discursive constructions, including appropriation, aestheticization, and
resistance.[22] Of these, several match to a remarkable degree constructions found in the writings of the earliest American foreign correspondents. What Spurr calls "appropriation," for example, intended as the
image of a foreign land as a chaos that awaits the colonizers' ordering
power, was found in the correspondence about several politically unstable countries (notably, Haiti and Mexico), well before the imperialistic
tendency of the United States began to dominate. A paradoxical corollary to this construction is the contradictory discourse that exalts tradi-
tional ways of life threatened by foreign (American) influence, all the
while suggesting that the influence has a civilizing effect; nineteenth-century correspondents writing about the picturesque Rhine
Valley constructed a similar discourse, which has come under criticism
in the twentieth century after the globalization of such American symbols as the McDonald's fast-food restaurant chain. Finally, a discourse
of resistance is present, identified by the journalists' questioning of
their own assumptions.

Returning to journalistic texts proper, discourse means, as Hall argued, dismissing the media model where media messages are transpar-
ent and the media themselves are "largely reflective or expressive of an
achieved consensus."[23] Consensus is no longer a natural phenomenon
but a "complex process of social construction and legitimation"; consequently, the media have an active role in consensus formation. The media, then, constitute the environment of the real and the common
sense, in what Hall defines as a movement "towards the winning of a
universal validity and legitimacy for accounts of the world which are
partial and particular, and towards the grounding of these particular
constructions in the taken-for-grantedness of the 'real.' "[24]

In other words, the media make things mean and in the process they
delegitimate alternative constructions and assist in maintaining a dominant discourse. This process is particularly crucial when the events to be
given meaning fall outside the "common sense"—which is precisely
what happens in foreign correspondence. The appropriation of the
event through discourse is the crucial and necessary condition for the
public's understanding of it; moreover, through discourse, the unknown becomes part of the "ideological inventory" of a society because
the unfamiliar is signified by references that are already part of that society's collective social knowledge.

The application of discourse theory to media discourse is of great political and social consequence. In the case of foreign correspondence, it not only suggests that one dominant discursive construction would be comparison with the American reality (a suggestion supported by findings in this research and presented later), but it also strongly hints at the constitutive responsibility of foreign correspondents for foreign policy and public attitudes toward it. Through their writings, the correspondents are virtually creating the "world" for American readers who then travel or even fight in it.

In sum, events and reality itself are not assumed to have intrinsic meanings that can be ascertained without frames of reference constituted in language, and these frames of reference are often representations found in the media. Thus, discourses are created that simplify and generate a common sense about whatever reality they give meaning to. Moreover, a discourse is often contradictory, embedding dominating constructions as well as the germs for paradigm shifts; it changes over time. Discourse has both a reflective and constitutive quality in regard to social practices. Discursive content is broadly ideological—it represents a summary, simplified, self-sustaining view of phenomena, though not necessarily one in direct support of existing power structures. However, the creation of a common sense can have immense consequences regardless of its link with dominating classes. These are the theoretical underpinnings of this study of the history of the creation of meaning for the American public of the world abroad.

In order to analyze discourse, to identify discursive constructions, cultural assumptions, and systems of beliefs, this study noted recurring themes and rhetorical structures. To quote Gunther Kress, "Discourse finds its expression in text."[25] In his view, the linguistic features of a text are determined not only by the conventions of a particular genre, but by the characteristics of the way subjects are "talked about." Because of this, linguistic features appear "as the sign of the system of meaning embodied in specific discourse" and therefore they have an ideological significance. In other words, Kress claims, ideological systems classify material in ways that are reflected in the organization of discourse and thus in the linguistic characteristics of a text.[26] Consequently, he infers that analyzing textual elements like whether an action is presented with a transitive or nontransitive verb leads to a discovery of the ideological position of such action within a particular discourse and ideological system.[27]

Such an analysis, however, needs corroboration from a similarly accurate analysis of the social context in which the text under examination is produced. For example, it seems inappropriate to infer the significance of American correspondents' discursive construction of a particular country only from the formal characteristics of the language used to describe it—though of course, once integrated with an analysis of other contextual elements, ranging from the journalistic practices of the time to the foreign policy toward that country, textual elements would provide strong clues as to the discourse of that correspondence. As Teun van Dijk notes, texts do not have meanings per se and thus, in order to understand how the meanings underlying the textual structures relate to the text, one needs to know the social, political, and cultural context of both text production and consumption.[28]

As already noted, such an approach is new to the study of foreign correspondence, as indeed is any systematic study of pioneering foreign correspondence. This book excludes the post-Civil War American imperialist period and all correspondence of war involving the United States, which literature on foreign correspondence all too often tends to focus on. The attempt here has been to try and identify a broader discourse in American newspapers' construction of foreign events, peoples, and cultures in the first two decades of organized foreign correspondence. War correspondence is somewhat anomalous to the purpose of this study, since it evokes a series of concerns—censorship, "rally around the flag" patriotism, a veritable extension of domestic correspondence when the country is involved in the conflict—that are assumed to significantly constrict and simplify the discursive constructions sought in this study. In fact, the scholarship's nearly exclusive focus on war or crisis reporting misleadingly identifies all foreign correspondence as political as opposed to more broadly cultural. The present study will begin to redress this imbalance, also because research suggested that foreign correspondence in the early period under scrutiny focused on cultural analysis.

With few exceptions,[29] most literature on international news and foreign correspondents focuses on the twentieth century, especially the post-Second World War era. One of its main concerns is the profession of foreign correspondent, studied through interviews and personal accounts of individual correspondents and the organizations they work for.[30] This includes memoirs, biographies, surveys, and "how-to" books.[31] Another focus of literature is the description of foreign news in the United States, including its provenance, the influences on its reporting and publication, and its history. Stephen Hess, in *International News and Foreign Correspondents*, thus establishes this concern: "What information about the world are we given by the mainstream media? How much? How good?"[32] He concludes, like many others, that the picture of the world given through American media is skewed at best. Mort Rosenblum, examining the kind of stories that get covered, concluded that foreign correspondents follow the rule of thumb that "all anyone cares about is coups and earthquakes"; he added that stories involving Americans or the United States have priority over others and that American reporters cover other countries according to cultural favoritism—concerns, as was found in this research, dating back to the earliest days of correspondence.[33]

Perhaps the most florid field of scholarship focuses on the flow of international news, ranging from censorship and propaganda to the ideology of objectivity, international relations, public policy, and the center-periphery world-order model.[34] This body of literature treats international news from a world-order perspective, focusing on the (unbalanced) flow of news from "center" to "periphery" and the consequences (at both the public and governmental levels) of such distorted coverage and distribution of information.[35] A related field of literature deals with media imperialism, or the cultural dominance and globalization consequent upon Western corporations' control over the flow of information.[36] Virtually none of these studies seeks a systematic historical development of foreign reporting.[37]

More relevant sources deal not with foreign correspondence per se, but with images of foreign nations in the United States—a concept integral to an understanding of constructions of foreign cultures. In the field of psychology, one scholar studied international images (defined as people's perceptions of other countries) and came to several conclusions significant to journalism. He found that the less information is available the more people rely on value-loaded images; specifically, his experiments suggest that people judge foreign countries based on two main types, "affluent ally" or "poor enemy," which is to say that "perceived political alignment and economic development are the two primary underlying dimensions" in judging foreign countries.[38]

Only three studies were found that investigated images of Europe in the period under study here, and all focused on the revolutions of 1848. Cushing Strout argued that Americans, throughout their history, have defined themselves in opposition to Europe.[39] Because, in Strout's view, Europe was perceived as "an alien stranger, a threatening enemy, and a potential pupil," Americans' attitude toward democratic movements in 1848 was ambivalent—they believed in "the American dream as an example for others only on the condition that it remain in actuality an exclusively American possession."[40] Arthur May concluded that American sympathy for European revolutionaries was engendered by remembrance of the American revolution and by nationalism that found expression in hostility against European despotism; however, he argued, nonintervention remained the official policy.[41] In a much more recent study, Timothy Roberts examined how American opinion of the revolutions helped shape American national identity (especially since the revolutions were put to partisan use by various national interests). He concluded that Americans perceived all revolutionary movements as one sweep, partly because of the lack of distinction in the way Americans received foreign news. Thus, they were most affected by the failure of the revolutions, a failure that reinforced a sense of American uniqueness and a policy of nonintervention.[42]

Returning to literature specific to nineteenth-century foreign correspondence, standard histories of journalism lack detail about early foreign correspondents. All the texts consulted agree that the first American editor to establish a regular corps of foreign correspondents in Europe was James Gordon Bennett of the *New York Herald*. He seized the opportunity presented by the 1838 technological innovation of steamboats crossing the Atlantic at much higher speeds than possible before[43] and sailed to Europe on the return trip of the first steamer to set up his news "bureaus."[44] Characteristically, he was quick in this innovation, for the steamer had arrived in New York on April 23 and on July 17 the *Herald* carried a letter from London from "one of our corps of European correspondents now organizing by Mr. Bennett."[45] Horace Greeley of the *New York Tribune* would also compete in the race for the best service from Europe in the 1840s, and by the late 1850s, Henry J. Raymond of the *New York Times* would apply the high standards of his newspaper to international reporting.[46]

What seems harder to pinpoint is the degree of demand for foreign news during the first half of the nineteenth century; in fact, journalism historians disagree as to whether foreign news was consistently prized or whether it actually declined after having been a staple of American newspapers throughout the colonial and revolutionary period.[47] It should also be noted that early foreign correspondence did not mean exclusively Europe to New York. George Wilkins Kendall, founder and editor of the *New Orleans Picayune*, was himself a correspondent during the 1846–1848 Mexican war (he was also in Paris from 1848–1856); Greeley sent Bayard Taylor as *Tribune* correspondent to Japan and China in the 1850s.[48]

A few leading figures in the history of foreign correspondence have been extensively studied (and are treated specifically in Chapter 2). James Gordon Bennett is one.[49] An 1855 "memoir" details his efforts to create a network of European journalists on his 1838 trip overseas, so that he could fulfill his vision for foreign news.[50] Horace Greeley's connection to foreign correspondence is somewhat less documented, with the major exception of his employing the first woman foreign correspondent, Margaret Fuller.[51] To her indeed belongs recognition as best documented and researched foreign correspondent for the period studied.

Finally, a word about the methods followed in this study. Eight newspapers were examined: Three New York papers, the *Herald* (founded in 1835, first to provide formally organized foreign correspondence), the *Tribune* (founded in 1841, edited by one of the century's defining journalists, Horace Greeley), and the *Times* (founded in 1851, generally considered a leader in foreign correspondence since its founding); from the Midwest, the *Chicago Tribune* (founded in 1847, leading daily for the region); from the West, the *St. Louis Missouri Republican* (founded in 1808, the state's leading paper and the chronicler of westward expansion); from New England, the *Boston Daily Evening Transcript* (founded in 1830; Boston was also for several years the northernmost terminus of the telegraph); and from the South, the *Charleston Daily Courier* (founded in 1800, the oldest newspaper in South Carolina and one that adopted aggressive news-gathering innovations) and the *New Orleans Picayune* (founded in 1837, and edited by George W. Kendall, a correspondent from Mexico and Europe in the 1840s–1850s). Issues were read for the years selected, which, based on attempts to maintain internal consistency and to avoid war periods, are 1838, 1845, 1852, and 1859.[52]

To establish how prevalent foreign news was, the amount of foreign news in the newspapers was measured and its percentage was calculated against the news hole. Foreign news is defined as any news item dealing with foreign matters, from reprinted digests and correspondence (excluding short stories, poems, literary notices, and editorials). The amount of news was measured in column inches.[53] To explore differences between reprinted digests and foreign correspondence, the former were compared with the latter in all eight newspapers. Data collected for the three New York newspapers and the *New Orleans Picayune* for 1838, 1845, and 1852 were integrated with data collected for all papers in 1859. For that year, two issues for the first week of every other month (January, March, May, July, September, November) were read—the same sampling used in all other inquiries. To study what may have been editors' constructions of other cultures, content of editorials was examined to identify any images of foreign cultures. This was assumed to provide insight about editors' frames of reference while they edited the correspondents' copy—keeping in mind that virtually all literature on foreign correspondents, albeit from the twentieth century, emphasizes how the lack of understanding and knowledge in the home office constitutes one of the major problems for foreign correspondence.[54]

To identify constructions in foreign policy of other cultures, the *Congressional Globe* was read (though its early records of congressional discussions are not verbatim), for discussion of two events that generated animated debates about foreign policy. The first, focused on the period from January 3 to February 27, 1845, is the annexation of the Republic of Texas, which had won independence from Mexico in 1836 and threatened to become an English ally. The issue dominated the 1844 presidential campaign and, when Congress voted to admit Texas, Mexico immediately broke relations with the United States (war between the two countries followed a year later). The second event is the discussion over government aid for the first laying of the Atlantic cable, between January and March 1857. The cable was laid in August 1858, allowing for instantaneous communication between England and the United States. It broke down in September, but for the twenty days it was working, it generated wide discussion about foreign relations and was heralded as the maker of world peace.

Generally, it should be emphasized that constructions were considered dominant only if they appeared in writings from or about different locales (for example, Italy and Barbados) and in newspapers conducted by different personalities and in different social and political milieus (for example, across sectional lines).

Finally, to examine possible differences in discursive constructions in the writings of women and African American correspondents, two different approaches were taken. For women, considering that bylines were rarely used in this period and therefore it would be hardly possible to discover the gender of correspondents selected at random from the newspapers, five articles of the correspondence of *New York Tribune* correspondent Margaret Fuller (1846–1850) were selected from the collection *These Sad but Glorious Days*; five more articles by Sara Jane Clarke (a.k.a. Grace Greenwood), correspondent in 1852–1853 for the *National Era* and the *Saturday Evening Post*, were selected from her collection, *Haps and Mishaps of a Tour in Europe*. Finally, five articles were found in the *New York Times* by correspondent Nancy Johnson (1857), identified by her signature A.J. and several secondary sources.

Extensive efforts to identify African American correspondents were unsuccessful. The only reference to one, T. Morris Chester as Liberia correspondent for the *New York Herald* before the Civil War, could not be corroborated by the author of the book in which that citation appeared, nor by sources read on the newspaper and on Chester.[55] Therefore, for the purpose of establishing whether alternative discourses of foreign cultures existed, foreign news and correspondence were read in Frederick Douglass' *North Star*, judged by several scholars the foremost black newspaper of the time and one containing news items comparable to those appearing in the mainstream press. While it cannot be ascertained with certainty whether *North Star* correspondents were black, foreign correspondence appearing in a black newspaper was deemed a likely locus of alternative discourses influenced by a black perspective.[56]

Large and diverse bodies of text were examined, and are quoted in this study, to familiarize both the researcher and the readers with the style and idiosyncrasies of mid-nineteenth-century foreign correspondence.

NOTES

1. *New Orleans Picayune*, June 28, 1863, p. 1.

2. James Carey, *Communication as Culture* (Boston: Unwin and Hyman, 1989): 15.

3. Daniel Goldhagen, *Hitler's Willing Executioners* (New York: Alfred A. Knopf, 1996).

4. *New York Herald*, November 6, 1845, p. 1.

5. Quoted in Norman Fairclough, *Media Discourse* (New York: Edward Arnold, 1995): 18 ff.

6. Stuart Hall, "The Rediscovery of 'Ideology': Return of the Repressed in Media Studies," in *Culture, Society and the Media*, Michael Gurevitch, Tony Bennett, James Curran, and Janet Woollacott, eds. (London: Methuen, 1982): 56–90.

7. These divisions are proposed by Sara Mills, *Discourse* (London and New York: Routledge, 1997). This book is the most recent comprehensive study of discourse.

8. Peter L. Berger and Thomas Luckmann, *The Social Construction of Reality: A Treatise in the Sociology of Knowledge* (Garden City, N.Y.: Doubleday, 1966): 1–18.

9. Berger and Luckmann, pp. 18–28.

10. Berger and Luckmann, pp. 34–40, 64–68.

11. Berger and Luckmann, pp. 109–128.

12. Berger and Luckmann, pp. 129–173.

13. Foucault, 1972, quoted in Mills, pp. 6–7.

14. Mills, p. 30.

15. Goldhagen, pp. 11–14.

16. Goldhagen, pp. 28–32.

17. Goldhagen, pp. 455–461.

18. See David Domke, *The Press, Social Change, and Race Relations in the Late Nineteenth Century*. Ph.D. dissertation, University of Minnesota, 1996, p. 6 ff.

19. David Spurr, *The Rhetoric of Empire* (Durham, N.C.: Duke University Press, 1993). For a brief examination of the use of discourse theory in colonial discourse theory, see also Mills, pp. 105–130. Some of her constructions, such as "othering" of the colonial subject through time-scale and sexual metaphor, are also found in Spurr's study.

20. Spurr, pp. 1–3.

21. Spurr, pp. 7–12.

22. Spurr, pp. 13–15.

23. Hall, pp. 59–61.

24. Hall, p. 65.

25. Gunther Kress, "Ideological Structures in Discourse," in Teun van Dijk, *Handbook of Discourse Analysis: Discourse Analysis in Society* (vol. 4) (London: Academic Press, 1985): 27.

26. Kress, p. 30.

27. Kress, pp. 34–41.

28. Teun van Dijk, "The Interdisciplinary Study of News as Discourse," in Klaus Bruhn Jensen and Nicholas W. Jankowski, eds., *A Handbook of Qualitative Methodologies for Mass Communication Research* (London: Routledge, 1991): 108–120.

29. Joyce Milton, *The Yellow Kids* (New York: Harper & Row, 1989), which details the adventures of foreign correspondents during the last decade of the nineteenth century. Ulf J. Bjork, "Sketches of Life and Society: Horace Greeley's Vision for Foreign Correspondence," *American Journalism* 14 (summer-fall 1997): 359–375.

30. In one instance, this approach has actually culminated in an oral history, unique, to the author's knowledge, in the field: Stephen MacKinnon and Oris Friesen, *China Reporting* (Berkeley: University of California Press, 1987).

31. For example, John C. Pollock, *The Politics of Crisis Reporting: Learning to be a Foreign Correspondent* (New York: Praeger, 1981), is based on interviews with correspondents based in Latin America and argues that the attitudes of foreign correspondents shape public and official responses.

32. Stephen Hess, *International News and Foreign Correspondents* (Washington, D.C.: Brookings Institution, 1996): 3.

33. Mort Rosenblum, *Coups and Earthquakes: Reporting the World for America* (New York: Harper & Row, 1979).

34. For overviews, see John C. Merrill, ed., *Global Journalism*, 2nd ed. (New York: Longman, 1991); Robert S. Fortner, *International Communication* (Belmont, Calif.: Wadsworth Publishing Company, 1993).

35. See, for example, John Lent, "Foreign News in American Media," *Journal of Communication* 27 (winter 1977); he found that foreign news is

often determined by international diplomacy and it is crisis-oriented. Also, UNESCO, "News Values and Principles of Cross-cultural Communication," *Reports and Papers on Mass Communication* 85, 1979; Jonathan Fenby, *The International News Services* (New York: Schocken Books, 1986) argues that the Third World would benefit from a "new world information order" that does away with the monopoly of Western news agencies.

36. John Tomlinson, *Cultural Imperialism: A Critical Introduction* (Baltimore: Johns Hopkins University Press, 1991).

37. An exception would be John Hohenberg, *Foreign Correspondence: The Great Reporters and Their Times.* 2nd ed. (Syracuse, N.Y.: Syracuse University Press, 1995); however, as the title implies, this work consists largely of narratives of individual reporters.

38. Seyda Turk, *Images of Foreign Nations*, Ph.D. dissertation, University of Washington, 1986.

39. Cushing Strout, *The American Image of the Old World* (New York: Harper & Row, 1963): 1, 18.

40. Strout, pp. 60–61.

41. Arthur J. May, *Contemporary American Opinion of the Mid-Century Revolutions in Central Europe*, Ph.D. dissertation, University of Pennsylvania, 1927).

42. Timothy M. Roberts, *The American Response to the European Revolutions of 1848*, Ph.D. dissertation, Oxford University, 1998.

43. Frederic Hudson, *Journalism in the United States from 1690 to 1872* (New York, Harper & Brothers, 1873): 450–451; James Lee, *History of American Journalism* (New York: Garden City Publishing Co., 1923): 199; Willard Bleyer, *Main Currents in the History of American Journalism* (Boston: Houghton Mifflin Company, 1927): 196; Alfred Lee, *The Daily Newspaper in America* (New York: Macmillan Co., 1937): 491; Frank Mott, *American Journalism* (New York: Macmillan Co., 1941): 244.

44. Hohenberg, p. 15, writes that Bennett's first six correspondents were in Paris, London, Glasgow, Berlin, Brussels, and Rome.

45. T.H. Giddings, "Rushing the Transatlantic News in the 1830s and 1840s," *New York Historical Society Quarterly*, 42 (January 1958): 49–59. James Lee (1923) also argues that Bennett had been interested in gathering foreign news since his founding of the *Herald*, for he announced in his policy, "We mean to procure intelligent correspondents in London, Paris, and Washington," p. 199.

46. Raymond had written in his prospectus for the *Times* that he intended to insert correspondence from Europe; Lee, James, p. 271.

47. Mott, p. 48, explains that the lack of timeliness of foreign news actually fit the model of news as records of historical events; he also contends that foreign news continued to be "given the place of honor" after the revolution, p. 114.

48. Hohenberg, pp. 17–19, 21.

49. See especially Don Seitz, *The James Gordon Bennetts* (Indianapolis: Bobbs-Merrill Co., 1928); Oliver Carlson, *The Man Who Made News* (New York: Duell, Sloan and Pearce, 1942); James Crouthamel, *Bennett's New York Herald and the Rise of the Popular Press* (Syracuse, N.Y.: Syracuse University Press, 1989).

50. Isaac Pray, *Memoirs of James Gordon Bennett and His Times* (New York: Arno, 1970): 235–252.

51. See Richard Kluger, *The Paper: The Life and Death of the New York Herald Tribune* (New York: Alfred A. Knopf, 1986): 59 ff.

52. For the *Chicago Tribune*, the first year read was 1853, not 1852, because no complete set of issues for 1852 was found, despite extensive research. Microfilm versions of the newspaper at the University of Florida and the University of Iowa, both prefaced by a 1968 note saying all extant copies of the *Tribune* were included, contained only seven scattered issues from April 1849 to December 1, 1852; since the latter date, all issues were included. For the year 1852, before December, only April 21 and May 6 were found. The University of Minnesota microfilm did not even contain the May 6 issue. The *Chicago Tribune* customer service advised that its print edition back issues are not held beyond 90 days, and the electronic archives only date back to 1985. Neither the Chicago Public Library nor the Chicago Historical Society had the complete set of issues. It seems likely, then, that there is in fact no extant complete set of issues for the paper before December 1, 1852. Moreover, a historian of the paper wrote that the early files were lost in the 1871 fire; Philip Kinsley, *The* Chicago Tribune, vol. 1 (New York: Alfred A. Knopf, 1943): 6.

53. To assess whether foreign news increased or decreased during those decades, three issues of each of the five newspapers founded by 1838 were examined for that year; three issues of the *New York Tribune*, the *Chicago Tribune*, and the *New York Times* were read for the first year they were considered in other parts of this research. Three issues of each of the eight newspapers were read for 1859. The issues read were, when available, the first Thursday for the months of January, July, and November. Because of the practical difficulties arising from the necessity to measure most of the newspaper issues on microfilm, and therefore with little knowledge of the actual sizes of newspapers for comparative purposes, it was deemed more efficient to calculate the percentage of foreign news versus the news hole for each issue selected, and then compare the percentages with other issues of the same and other papers.

54. Two issues for the first week of every other month were read for all newspapers in 1838 and 1859, and data randomly collected from 1845 and 1852 were also integrated.

55. Armistead S. Pride and Clint C. Wilson II, *A History of the Black Press* (Washington, D.C.: Howard University Press, 1997): 170. Dr. Wilson could not find where the reference to Chester came from; he added that much of

Pride's original source references have been lost and his papers at the Moorland-Spingarn Research Center at Howard University do not contain information about Chester as foreign correspondent. Dr. Wilson also wrote in a personal communication that he was not aware of any black foreign correspondents in the first half of the nineteenth century. Chester's biography, in R.J.M. Blackett, ed., *Thomas Morris Chester, Black Civil War Correspondent: His Dispatches from the Virginia Front* (Baton Rouge: University of Louisiana Press, 1989), reports that Chester was in Liberia for several periods between 1853 and 1860, and that he wrote for the *Colonization Herald*, but makes no mention of any relation with the *New York Herald*. Nor does Chester's entry in the American National Biography, vol. 4. Karen Beavers, reference librarian at the University of Minnesota's Wilson Library, kindly helped in this stage of research and found no mention of black correspondents in the following indexes: Black Studies Database, American History and Life, and Humanities Citation Index. Research in other histories of the black press and in general histories of journalism did not discover black correspondents either.

56. The first six months of continuing issues, December 1847 to June 1848, were read, as well as all extant scattered issues from November 1849 to April 1851, when the paper's last issue appeared, to identify discourses and discursive constructions about foreign cultures. All items dealing with foreign affairs were examined, including editorials, news digests, and foreign correspondence.

CHAPTER 2

EARLY AMERICAN JOURNALISM AND NEWS FROM ABROAD

The beginning of formally organized foreign correspondence happened during a revolutionary period in American journalism; indeed, between 1820 and 1860, journalism underwent a radical transformation. The 1830s signal the rise of the penny press and the introduction of a new model of journalism—most significantly, the focus of newspapers began to shift from presenting the editors and their party's views to selling news as a commodity. In this milieu, the newsroom began to be differentiated, the reporter emerged as a professional with responsibilities different from the editors', and the ethic of objectivity was tentatively introduced. Moreover, the rapid diffusion of technological innovations—from the perspective of foreign correspondence, especially steamboat ocean transportation and the telegraph—contributed to new ways of gathering, transmitting, presenting, and delivering the news.

Historians point to September 3, 1833, when Benjamin Day published the first issue of the *New York Sun*, as the beginning of this new era in American journalism. The 1820s had been the high point of the party press, when newspapers were understood as politicians' necessary tools to move the electorate.[1] Financially and philosophically inextricably linked to parties, the newspapers of the Jacksonian era circulated among a small, elite group of subscribers. Most of the editorial content, in fact, consisted of editorials and political debates; the only real news was foreign news, not domestic or local.[2]

The appearance of the cheap, street-distributed, general interest *Sun* and similar penny papers that followed it (so called because they cost a penny, or about a sixth of the price of party papers) altered the face of journalism and its social role. Those papers were by no means apolitical—most journalists apparently didn't conceptualize their role as truly nonpolitical until well after the Civil War, and politics and partisanship continued to command the editors' attention throughout the period studied here.[3] Nor did politics diminish in importance as crucial newspaper content; according to one scholar, politics remained the top category of news between 1820 and 1860.[4]

Nevertheless, the penny newspapers did introduce pivotal changes, of which the most significant to this study of foreign correspondence are the introduction of the reporter and the shift in focus from ideas to events, about which reporters gathered information.[5] Changes on the production side also mirrored changes in how and where the newspapers were received—cheap prices and concise, captivating, often sensationalistic content attracted an increasingly large readership, and the expanding network of communications diversified the audience geographically. Advertisers took notice, and advertising came to substitute political patronage as the press' financial base.[6]

Several scholars highlight the penny press' social role as informer and entertainer of the masses, rooting it in the democratizing movement of the era.[7] Particularly one sociologist, Michael Schudson, has dubbed the penny press a "middle-class institution."[8] He argued that papers like the *New York Herald* and the *New York Tribune* did not emerge because of advances in communications or increasing literacy in classes demanding simpler content—although these changes facilitated the emergence of the penny press. His explanation revolves on what he identifies as a time of egalitarianism, though principally linked to the market interests of the middle class. Schudson also sees the beginning of objectivity—as a belief in facts rather than a deference to opinions—as related to this development toward democratization, which included news content as well.[9] Content focused on "human interest" stories, which often meant the violent and trivial presented in a flippant tone, though by the 1850s the penny press had begun to outgrow sensationalism, while not neglecting its mass readership.

David Mindich, who studied the development of objectivity in the nineteenth century, also noted that the penny papers were the first to embrace two characteristics of objectivity—detachment and nonpartisanship (in the sense of nonaffiliation with a party).[10] Similarly, James Lee and Hudson argued that the penny press signaled the beginning of an independent press focused on the news.[11] Dan Schiller interrelates the commercialization of newspapers, the progressive introduction of objectivity, and the division of newsroom labor as factors in the nascent professionalization of journalism, marked by the appearance of reporters and correspondents. He argued that by the mid-nineteenth century, news was beginning to be identified as "the product of a skilled endeavor."[12]

While the New York penny press, and most notably the *Herald*, the *Tribune*, and the *Times*, led the way in these changes, and while, by 1840, the largest American cities had penny papers,[13] one scholar has cautioned against considering the New York penny papers as representative of the American press in general before 1860. Shaw's research did not find papers on average to have become more responsive to their popular audiences, nor more social in content. However, he did find a development of the reporter as a professional as well as an increased speed of news dissemination (measured in the time to gather news, to move it nationally and internationally, and in the total time elapsed between an event and the publication of its report).[14]

In this milieu of focus on news as events and increasingly enterprising news-gathering, it is only fitting that editors should realize the importance of sending correspondents abroad to report foreign news in person. In fact, the competition for foreign news was only accelerated by the changing conceptualization of journalism and by technological advances. Before Bennett's efforts in 1838, there was no organized European correspondence[15]—but this didn't mean that there was a lack of competition for the fastest procurement of foreign news. Interestingly, the developments of foreign correspondence and of more efficient systems to receive news from foreign newspapers were not exclusionary—while correspondents increasingly sent personal accounts from abroad, editors continued to race to be the first with reprinted news, which eventually became the nearly exclusive domain of The Associated Press.

Before the advent of transatlantic steamships, editors competed for foreign news via "newsboats," small vessels with which editors approached incoming ships, secured packets of European or South American papers, and raced back to print the news.[16] Samuel Topliff first started this kind of news enterprise in 1811 to gather foreign news for the reading room at his Exchange Coffee House in Boston; only two years later, Aaron Smith Willington, owner of the *Charleston Courier*, had slaves row him to meet arriving ships and thus secured the "scoop" of the treaty of Ghent (between Great Britain and the United States) in 1815.[17] By the 1820s, the innovation had reached the New York harbor, probably introduced by Bennett, who had worked with Willington.[18]

A new era was heralded by Samuel Cunard's steamship service between Liverpool and Boston in the late 1830s. Since the boats usually made their first call at Halifax, Nova Scotia, several New York editors established complex relays from the Canadian outpost to New York, employing carrier pigeons, horse expresses, special vessels, the railroad, and eventually the telegraph to be the first with news from European papers.[19] By 1847, Halifax and Portland were linked by wire and news-gatherers raced for telegraph offices, not boats. Just a year later in 1848, the editors of the six most prominent New York papers (the *Sun, Herald, Journal of Commerce, Courier and Enquirer, Tribune,* and *Express*) pooled their resources and joined in a cooperative to gather foreign news from the ships at Halifax and Boston—their association would later be named The Associated Press.[20] The AP's first news-gathering efforts were to intercept European news at Halifax, take it to Boston (the northernmost telegraph terminal) and then transmit it over the wire to New York.[21] The cooperative also used a news yacht to approach the ships before they arrived at port.[22]

At first, the cooperative had one powerful rival in Halifax. Daniel Craig had been distributing foreign news via carrier pigeons to papers all over the Eastern seaboard states, including the *New York Herald,* his most important client.[23] Indeed, Bennett had been paying Craig a $500 bonus for each hour the *Herald* received European news before its New York competition.[24] But by 1849, the telegraph extended from New York to Halifax and St. John, New Brunswick, rendering Craig's pigeons obsolete; and cooperation again prevailed over competition. Craig was hired by the AP and became its first foreign correspondent in Halifax and then, in 1851, its general agent.[25] Under his leadership, the AP included a seventh member, the just-founded *New York Times* (whose editor, Henry J. Raymond, had been a sponsor of the cooperative since its founding in his capacity as managing editor of the *Courier and Enquirer*). The seven members acted as equal partners and admitted other papers as clients for their foreign news services.[26]

Thus, The Associated Press became the major conveyor of foreign news to American newspapers. In 1860, a telegraph operator said newspapers "could not do without the earliest foreign news, and they could not get it except from Craig."[27] One student of the American wire services argued that the AP even influenced the style and subject matter of its clients, over whom it exerted great control.[28] But never, in the period studied, was the AP a source of foreign correspondence. Indeed, aside from Craig's employment at Halifax, the AP did not send an American reporter abroad until 1866, when the Atlantic cable started functioning and the AP London bureau was established.[29] Rather, the AP only received foreign news from the existing European news agencies, especially Agence Havas in France, Wolff's service in Germany, and Reuters in England, which were not cooperatives but private commercial enterprises that originally served also governmental agencies and businesses. In 1859, Craig entered the AP in a global pact with those agencies, a pact that was reinforced in 1870 in the "agency cartel" that divided the world into four news-reporting zones, with the AP responsible for reporting in the United States only.[30] Through the arrangement with the European agencies, the AP became a monopoly in the distribution of foreign news in the United States.[31]

By the late 1850s, as discussed in Chapter 3, virtually identical digests of foreign news, mostly extracted from foreign newspapers, collected and telegraphed by The Associated Press, were printed in the major newspapers of New York and nationwide. But while this system seems to have alleviated the editors' competition in the realm of reprinted foreign news, a new field had opened up for newspaper enterprise—foreign correspondence. The questions of how the correspondence differed from the digests and what the correspondents wrote about their new occupation are addressed in Chapter 3. How the realm of foreign correspondence expanded after Bennett's pioneering efforts is treated below, especially in regard to the newspapers selected for this study.

The birth of foreign correspondence seems a logical development stemming from the 1830s burgeoning editorial focus on news, the competition for foreign news, and the increasing importance of reporters, although it has not been studied in depth from this perspective. As noted above, the *New York Herald* was the first to enlist regular foreign correspondents, six in Europe in 1838 (in Paris, London, Glasgow, Berlin, Brussels, and Rome) and later several more in Mexico and Canada; the *New York Sun* followed with a London correspondent in 1843.[32] The *Herald* also syndicated its foreign correspondence, earning great popularity through reprints.[33] In the 1840s, the *Boston Atlas* and the *Daily Chronotype*, the *New Orleans Picayune*, the *Albany Evening Journal*, the *United States Gazette*, the *Saturday Evening Post* and the *American* in Philadelphia, and the *National Intelligencer* in Washington sent correspondents abroad.[34] By 1850, the *New York Tribune*, founded in 1841 by Horace Greeley, had four European correspondents, two in Canada, and one each in Mexico, Cuba, and Central America.[35]

Very little information is available about these correspondents, with the exception of those editors who themselves went abroad at some time as reporters. In fact, to identify all of these correspondents, considering that bylines were used very sparingly at the time, is impossible. A few of the writers, especially in the earliest years, were not Americans. For example, an Irishman, Dionysius Lardner, was Bennett's first Paris correspondent.[36] However, several other correspondents were Americans; for example, the *New Orleans Picayune* editor employed John D. Osborn of Virginia as a Paris correspondent, who wrote under the pen name "Gamma."[37] Even where no biographical information is known, it is sometimes possible to establish from the correspondence itself whether the writers were Americans or not, from references such as one to the U.S. government as "our Government" and one to "our hotels" in a comparison between British and American hospitality.[38] Overall, for the purposes of this study, unless otherwise specified, the correspondents were assumed to be Americans.

The correspondence specifically is best treated in the context of the individual newspapers, which were examined in this study for the discourses of foreign cultures. The *New York Herald* was the first, and for years the best, with foreign correspondence.[39] Founded in 1835 by Bennett, the *Herald* experienced an almost immediate success; Bennett capitalized on sensational news, especially violent crime, but quickly used the characteristically aggressive news-gathering attitude in business, sports, society news as well as in editorials. By 1860, with a circulation of 77,000, the *Herald* was the world's largest daily.[40] It was also the best-known American newspaper in Europe, where in 1856 its international edition had a circulation of 2,000 copies.[41]

Bennett was, in a sense, his own first foreign correspondent—sending dispatches from Europe when he traveled there to organize his corps of correspondents.[42] The first letter from one of his correspondents, from London, reported on the state of commerce in England, especially the Bank of England;[43] the same correspondent, or another, was in London throughout 1838, reporting business news, as did another correspondent from Liverpool, who also covered maritime news.[44] That Bennett should concern himself with business news first follows from his vision of news-gathering, as appears in one of his 1838 letters from Europe:

I must continue, day after day, to give . . . correct and accurate sketches or analyses of the great money market here, because I know that although we are both religious and sentimental, we are also very scientific in the matter of the purse.

. . . I was the first editor who established a daily money market report in the United States, in the face of one of the most bitter oppositions that man could encounter . . . before I return to New York, I will organize and establish some of the greatest monetary, commercial, and general correspondence that any American paper ever had. . . . I shall make it a point, therefore, to seek out and establish a *corps* of correspondents, such as have never been attached to a New York paper.[45]

By 1840, the *Herald* employed a dozen foreign correspondents. Bennett expanded his network of correspondence after another visit abroad in 1847, including Istanbul (then Constantinople) and Bombay as areas to be covered; he had bureaus in Liverpool, Paris, Antwerp, and Bremen, and correspondents in London, Brussels, Vienna, Munich, Trieste, Berne, Rome, Madrid, Naples, and Alexandria. Though Bennett personally focused on Europe in his travels, he also prided himself on extensive correspondence from Central and South America.[46]

In addition to his ardent interest in foreign correspondence, Bennett had another strong connection with things abroad—he was the most vocal supporter of the United States' expansionist foreign policy in American journalism.[47] His patriotism, or jingoism, influenced his editorials and his own correspondence, as will be further discussed in later chapters; Mindich argued this contributed to the *Herald*'s success.[48] Bennett took plenty of opportunities to show his Anglophobia, especially when British interests threatened America, as in the border squabbles with Canada and the annexations of Oregon and Texas. He agitated in the 1840s for the annexation of Mexico and throughout the 1850s for the purchase of Cuba, firmly believing that the United States was the best country in the world and that other countries would benefit from incorporation; he thus made the *Herald* the bearer of Manifest Destiny sentiments.[49] Nevertheless, the *Herald* covered extensively foreign policy issues and foreign affairs, and, aside from its editorial stance, its foreign correspondence has been praised for perceptiveness and breadth of coverage.[50]

Another New York penny paper soon rose to a renown equal to, if not greater than, that of the *Herald*—the *New York Tribune*, founded in 1841 by Horace Greeley, one of the most influential editors in the nineteenth century. By 1860, the paper had a circulation of 55,000 copies, and its weekly edition sold about 200,000 copies.[51] Greeley, despite his early affiliation with the conservative Whig party, was a great

believer in the potential of justice for all represented by American democracy and supported several reforms, including abolition, temper-
ance, and women's civil rights. He has been credited with lifting the
penny press from sensationalism to an intellectually stimulating level,
without losing readership.[52]

The trademark of the *Tribune* were its editorials, which commanded
attention nationwide and through which Greeley fought for society's
improvements.[53] But Greeley also introduced a new model of foreign
correspondence, both in the way he envisioned it and in the personalities he hired as special correspondents—including Margaret Fuller
(whose correspondence is discussed in Chapter 6), Karl Marx (between
1851–1861), and America's perhaps most famous nineteenth-century
travel writer, Bayard Taylor. Greeley himself traveled to Europe in
1851, and his book of the correspondence from the trip reveals his increasing admiration for American egalitarian institutions compared to
what he saw as the despotism of European regimes.[54] In the preface to
the book, Greeley wrote that he intended, through his correspondence, "to give a clear and vivid daguerreotype of the districts I tra-
versed and the incidents which came under my observation," and he
apologized for the "crude and rash" appearance of his opinions about
national character, especially of Italy, which he feared might offend Italians settled in the United States.[55]

If Greeley's trust in American superiority is similar to Bennett's, one
scholar argues that Greeley's vision of foreign correspondence signaled
a departure from what had come before. Bjork suggests that Greeley's
training as a magazine journalist (for the weekly *New-Yorker*, which
ceased publication in 1841) influenced him to envision foreign correspondence as more akin to travel letters than to reprinted news digests.
While the *Tribune* treated foreign news as did other newspapers of the
time, it separated foreign news from correspondence, which Greeley
valued more for its descriptive and moral value than for the news value.
But his correspondents were instructed to be more than travel writers
and to discuss foreign countries' social and political environments, all
the while remaining focused on personal experience. However, already
in the mid-1840s, this model of correspondence competed with the
more factually-oriented kind, which eventually dominated the *Tribune*
in the 1860s.[56] Both models, as discussed below, were found in this
study of discourses, and indeed most correspondence read in the *Tribune* and the other papers reflected the kind of descriptive, analytical,
in-depth style Greeley apparently championed. In Greeley's words
about the correspondent known by the initials W.W., "Our European

Correspondent . . . travels under express instructions from us to make himself acquainted with the People [abroad], their modes of life and thought, their feelings, hardships, hopes and antipathies."[57]

For literary, yet analytical correspondence, Greeley picked the likes of Charles A. Dana, who later in the 1860s became the celebrated editor of the *New York Sun*, and Bayard Taylor. Dana, after 1849 managing editor of the *Tribune*, reported on the 1848 revolutions in Europe, traveling in the principal capital cities of Berlin, Paris, and London. His words in a *Tribune* essay on the American journalist, who "regards nothing with indifference," echo Greeley's precepts:

[A journalist] carries with him a degree of genuine sympathy in the event and its actors which renders him an excellent observer and reporter. He is no dull analyzer, and sees the thing before he attempts to speculate on its philosophy and consequences. . . . [H]is enthusiasm—of which he has a large stock—concentrates itself upon persons and deeds and makes him almost a part of the occurrence he describes. His element is action and his method rapidity.[58]

But it is Taylor who embodied the model of the correspondent as insightful travel writer, providing the *Tribune* with beautifully written correspondence from Europe, beginning in 1844, and later from more exotic locales. In 1852 he was sent to cover the excavation of Nineveh (in Iraq) and to travel in the Nile Valley; at the end of that trip, while in Istanbul, he was ordered to proceed to the coast of China, where he boarded Commodore Matthew Perry's fleet, on its way to open trade with Japan.[59]

Taylor is considered to have had a particular way of engaging his readers by participating in the cultures he described—though he was inclined to admire a country's heritage and art, while disparaging the native people, an attitude that made for ambivalent correspondence (treated later here in discussion of discourses of foreign cultures). He also often compared what he saw to the United States, which of course he held as the epitome of freedom and respect for individual rights. Incidentally, so did most other nineteenth-century travel writers, for whom travel was a means of seeking a cultural identity, and their comparisons with the United States were mostly patriotic. For most of his career, Taylor was reputed to be the best travel writer in the United States.[60]

By the early 1850s, the *Herald* and the *Tribune* had a powerful competitor in the field of foreign correspondence—the *New York Times*, edited by Henry J. Raymond. Even though the *Times* trailed both other papers with a circulation of 35,000 by 1860, it was intended since its inception to elevate journalism to a higher level. The *Times* achieved this goal with an unprecedented emphasis on fairness and balanced, thorough reporting that strove for nonpartisan objectivity, even though Raymond was deeply involved in politics. Since he founded the paper, Raymond also sought to achieve excellence in foreign correspondence.[61]

News from Europe occupied three and a half columns of the front page of the first number of the *Times*.[62] Raymond traveled to England in 1853 to arrange for special correspondence;[63] the editor had an outstanding foreign correspondent in the person of William E. Johnston, writing under the pen name "Malakoff" and based in Paris at least after January 1857.[64] With Johnston, Raymond himself reported on the war that France and Italy waged against the Austrian empire in 1859—and they managed to secure the greatest foreign correspondence scoop of the time. Like Bennett before him, Raymond was, at the beginning, his paper's most famous foreign correspondent.

The editor sailed for France, where his family was living, in May 1859; there he rejoined Johnston and with him made his way to the battlefields of Savoy (now Piedmont) and Lombardy in northern Italy, eager to follow the armies to the front.[65] He arrived in time to witness the bloodiest and decisive battle in the war, the Battle of Solferino, on June 24, in which 30,000 soldiers died as the French–Sardinian army gave the final push in driving the Austrians out of Italy. Raymond and Johnston were the only American reporters at the front, where they witnessed the carnage for twelve hours before the Austrians retreated in the evening. All night long, Raymond and Johnston wrote their dispatches, on which Raymond placed great hopes—he wanted his account of Solferino to reach New York before the British papers containing that of the *London Times* correspondent. Thanks to Johnston's friendships in the French army, the correspondent was able to give the reports to an imperial courier leaving for Paris. Raymond's wife got them three days later in Paris and she took them to the port of Le Havre, where a steamship was about to sail for New York. Thus, when Raymond's and Malakoff's articles appeared in the *New York Times* on July 12, they were the first eyewitness account of the battle in the American press.[66]

Another American editor who had gone abroad to get firsthand reports of a war was George Wilkins Kendall, founder of the *New Orleans Picayune*. He was the greatest war correspondent in the conflict against Mexico in 1846. The *Picayune*, started in 1837, was the first penny newspaper in the South; not only was it the first paper in New Orleans sold for less than a dime, but it also followed the *New York Sun* and the

New York Herald in its small format, light tone, and emphasis on "human interest" stories.[67] The paper was established as the principal source of news regarding the annexation of Texas, for its correspondents quickly went to the territory and the main ports of Mexico.[68] Kendall, who had already been in Mexico as part of an ill-fated Texan expedition to conquer the country, covered all the major battles of the war and beat the War Department couriers with the news of the peace treaty in 1848.

Kendall also went to Europe in 1848, covering the revolutions there and sending dispatches to New Orleans from London, Paris, Hamburg, and Brussels.[69] In the decade of 1850–1860, the *Picayune* had correspondents in several European capitals. "Gamma" in Paris, for example, furnished the paper with wide coverage of international affairs. Nevertheless, Kendall continued to provide correspondence from Europe until 1856, when he moved to a sheep ranch in Texas, a state he ardently supported for annexation.[70]

Much less information is available about the other papers selected for study of foreign correspondence, or about their own correspondents. The *Charleston Courier*, founded in 1803, was the oldest newspaper in South Carolina. Its connection with foreign news enterprise has been noted above, and indeed aggressive news-gathering was a characteristic of the paper. One of its reporters, Samuel Knapp, was in Washington in 1827 to cover Congress, and he, with only two other journalists (one of whom was Bennett), inaugurated continuing press coverage of the nation's capitol. During the Mexican war, the *Courier* pooled resources with the *Picayune* and several other papers to establish an express system to deliver battlefield news from New Orleans to New York.[71] Editorially, the *Courier* supported the Unionist Party during the nullification crisis.[72]

Another older paper included in this study of foreign correspondence is the *Boston Transcript*, founded in 1830 and considered a precursor of the penny press.[73] At first, it contained little local news, while most of its foreign and national news was reprinted from other papers; its most solid beat was arts and culture. Editorially, it appealed to the conservative classes and sympathized with the Whig Party.[74] For five years, between 1842 and 1847, it was edited by Cornelia Walter, the sister of the paper's founder. She became the first woman to edit a major daily. In 1848, the *Transcript* editor joined those of eight other Boston papers in buying a service of foreign news from the telegraph company; a staff writer eulogized the Atlantic cable when it operated for a short time in 1858.[75]

Finally, two Midwestern papers were also becoming established on the national scene. The *Missouri Republican* was founded in 1808 in St. Louis, which, until the late 1850s, was the metropolis of the Northwest.[76] The *Republican*, which was actually Democratic, was the state's leading paper, gaining a wide readership especially through its weekly edition, and it was considered the chronicler of the expansion in the West.[77] Destined to overshadow the *Republican*, just as Chicago overshadowed St. Louis, was the *Chicago Tribune*, founded in 1847. The paper has been most closely studied for its role in the emergence on the political scene of Abraham Lincoln, but it has also been considered representative of the spirit of the West.[78]

The *Chicago Tribune* changed hands several times and enjoyed a very small circulation in its early years; it began to be a solid presence in journalism only after Joseph Medill took the editorship in 1855. Its first telegraphic dispatch, received in 1848, was about foreign news, the French revolution. However, by the winter of 1852–1853, the *Tribune* editor promised letters from correspondents in Great Britain, France, and Italy; by the late 1850s, its influence, unchallenged in the West, was equal to that of New York's leading dailies. Circulation, however, remained low by New York standards, counting 4,000 copies of the daily edition and 8,000 of the weekly in 1857. After 1858, the *Tribune* was devoted to promoting the cause of the Republican Party and eventually of Lincoln.[79]

Expanding newspapers, with enterprising editors eager to fulfill their interest in foreign news with quicker transmission of intelligence from abroad and to bring fresher, more insightful accounts of foreign realities, provide the essential background to this study of the first American foreign correspondents.

NOTES

1. Gerald J. Baldasty, *The Commercialization of News in the Nineteenth Century* (Madison: University of Wisconsin Press, 1992): 11–35.

2. Willard G. Bleyer, *Main Currents in the History of American Journalism* (Boston: Houghton Mifflin Company, 1927): 152–153.

3. Hazel Dicken-Garcia, *Journalistic Standards in Nineteenth-Century America* (Madison: University of Wisconsin Press, 1989): 46–47.

4. Donald L. Shaw, "At the Crossroads: Change and Continuity in American Press News, 1820–1860," *Journalism History* 8:2 (1981): 49.

5. Dicken-Garcia, pp. 41–42.

6. Baldasty argued the commercialization of news was the driving force behind the growth of the penny press, p. 58.

7. Bleyer, p. 155.

8. Michael Schudson, *Discovering the News* (New York: Basic Books, Inc. 1978): 13.

9. Schudson, p. 60.

10. David T.Z. Mindich, *Just the Facts* (New York: New York University Press, 1998): 12.

11. James M. Lee, *History of American Journalism* (New York: Garden City Publishing Co., 1923): 205; Frederic Hudson, *Journalism in the United States* (New York: Harper & Brothers, 1873): 427.

12. Dan Schiller, "An Historical Approach to Objectivity and Professionalism in American News Reporting," *Journal of Communication*, 29 (1979): 46–57.

13. Michael Emery, Edwin Emery, and Nancy L. Roberts, *The Press and America*. 9th ed. (Boston: Allyn and Bacon, 2000): 105.

14. Shaw, pp. 38–49.

15. Hudson, p. 451.

16. T.H. Giddings, "Rushing the Transatlantic News in the 1830s and 1840s," *The New York Historical Society Quarterly*, 42: 1, January 1958, pp. 50–51.

17. Victor Rosewater, *History of Cooperative News-Gathering in the United States* (New York: D. Appleton and Co., 1930): 5–10.

18. Giddings, p. 52.

19. Giddings, pp. 54–55.

20. Giddings, pp. 58–59. Rosewater concurs that "the expedition of foreign news was the prime object" of the founding of the AP; p. 66.

21. Oliver Gramling, *AP: The Story of News* (Port Washington, N.Y.: Kennikat Press, 1940): 20.

22. "The [steamship] Vigo . . . passed Cape Race at 3 o'clock on the morning of the 3d inst., where she was boarded by the news yacht of the Associated Press, and summary of her news obtained," *New York Tribune*, July 7, 1859, p. 5.

23. Frank L. Mott, *American Journalism* (New York: Macmillan Co., 1941): 246.

24. Menahem Blondheim, *News Over the Wires* (Cambridge, Mass.: Harvard University Press, 1994): 19.

25. Gramling, pp. 26–28.

26. Rosewater, p. 87; Gramling, p. 31.

27. Quoted in Blondheim, p. 96.

28. Richard A. Schwarzlose, *The American Wire Services: A Study of Their Development as a Social Institution* (New York: Arno Press, 1979): 40, 102.

29. Gramling, pp. 69–70.

30. John Hohenberg, *Foreign Correspondence: The Great Reporters and Their Times*. 2nd ed. (Syracuse, N.Y.: Syracuse University Press, 1995):

12–13. He argues that the AP did not have regular foreign correspondents until the twentieth century, pp. 63–64.

31. Jonathan Fenby, *The International News Services* (New York: Schocken Books, 1986): 26–27; Hohenberg, p. 12; Blondheim, p. 117.

32. Robert Desmond, *The Press and World Affairs* (New York: D. Appleton-Century Co., 1937): 16–17.

33. Hohenberg, p. 15.

34. Giddings, p. 50.

35. Desmond, p. 19.

36. Desmond, p. 19; Hohenberg, p. 15.

37. Thomas E. Dabney, *One Hundred Great Years* (Baton Rouge: Louisiana State University Press, 1944): 106.

38. Correspondence of the *New York Times*, in the *Charleston Courier*, March 3, 1859, p. 1; *Missouri Republican*, September 1, 1859, p. 2.

39. James M. Lee, p. 200.

40. Emery, Emery, and Roberts, p. 102.

41. James L. Crouthamel, *Bennett's New York Herald and the Rise of the Popular Press* (Syracuse, N.Y.: Syracuse University Press, 1989): 56.

42. Hohenberg, p. 15.

43. *New York Herald*, July 17, 1838, with the preface, "[an] important letter from one of our *corps* of European correspondents, now organizing by Mr. Bennett."

44. July 25, 1838, p. 2; December 8, 1838, p. 4; July 26, 1838, p. 2 (from "one of our Liverpool correspondents," the article described a new steamer, the first "direct steam conveyance" between New York and Liverpool).

45. *Herald*, July 19 and July 20, 1838, p. 2.

46. Crouthamel, pp. 49–51.

47. Crouthamel, p. 56 ff.

48. Mindich, p. 48.

49. Crouthamel, pp. 56–66.

50. Crouthamel, pp. 68, 162.

51. Richard Kluger, *The Paper* (New York: Alfred A. Knopf, 1986): 92.

52. Emery, Emery, and Roberts, pp. 105–107.

53. Kluger, p. 75.

54. Martha Pallante, "Horace Greeley," in *Dictionary of Literary Biography, vol. 189: American Travel Writers, 1850–1915* (Detroit: Gale Research, 1998): 133–135.

55. Horace Greeley, *Glances at Europe: In a Series of Letters from Great Britain, France, Italy, Switzerland &c., during the Summer of 1851. Including Notices of the Great Exhibition, or World's Fair* (New York: Dewitt & Davenport, 1851): iv–vi.

56. Ulf Bjork, "Sketches of Life and Society," *American Journalism*, 14, summer-fall 1997, 365–375.

57. *Tribune*, January 29, 1844, p. 2; quoted in Bjork, p. 373.

58. Kluger, p. 71.

59. Hohenberg, pp. 21–22; Kluger, p. 74.

60. James L. Gray, "Bayard Taylor," in *Dictionary of Literary Biography*, *vol. 189: American Travel Writers, 1850–1915* (Detroit: Gale Research, 1998): 321–335; James Schramer and Donald Ross, eds., "Introduction," *Dictionary of Literary Biography, vol. 183: American Travel Writers, 1776–1864* (Detroit: Gale Research, 1997): xv–xxv.

61. Emery, Emery, and Roberts, pp. 107–108; James M. Lee, p. 271; Mott, p. 280.

62. Elmer Davis, *History of the New York Times* (New York: The New York Times, 1921): 24–25.

63. Francis Brown, *Raymond of the Times* (New York: W.W. Norton, 1951): 123.

64. Davis, p. 42.

65. For the account of Raymond in Italy, see Brown, pp. 169–179.

66. An editorial in the paper duly noted that Paris and London newspapers received did not have the accounts of Solferino, and therefore the *New York Times* editors had "the pleasure of laying before our readers this morning the first complete and accurate details of the great battle," *New York Times*, July 12, 1859, p. 4. Raymond's and Malakoff's letters occupied the whole front page of the July 12, 1859, edition, as well as nearly four columns on p. 8.

67. Dabney, pp. 15–16.

68. Fayette Copeland, *Kendall of the Picayune* (Norman: University of Oklahoma Press, 1943): 124.

69. Dabney, pp. 81–82.

70. Dabney, pp. 92, 106.

71. Emery, Emery, and Roberts, pp. 110, 115.

72. Mott, p. 189.

73. James M. Lee, p. 185.

74. Joseph E. Chamberlin, *The Boston Transcript* (Boston: Houghton Mifflin Company, 1930): 20–23.

75. Chamberlin, pp. 96, 123.

76. Mott, p. 283.

77. Hudson, p. 202.

78. Philip Kinsley, *The* Chicago Tribune, vol. 1 (New York: Alfred A. Knopf, 1943): 5.

79. Kinsley, pp. 9, 11, 20, 33, 59, 90.

CHAPTER 3

THE SHAPING OF FOREIGN NEWS: IMPROVING ON THE SINGLE ELECTRICIAN AT A SEAPORT TOWN

Between 1838 and 1859, foreign news increased in the newspapers studied and was a source of pride (and competitiveness) for their editors. Foreign news took two forms: The digests, eventually streamlined by The Associated Press, were mostly written in what today is known as "straight" news style and lacked context, background, and analysis. Because they tended to focus on news of conflict or the sensational, they might have fostered an image of the world as a dangerous, strange place. The other form of foreign news was foreign correspondence, which both editors and correspondents seemed to have envisioned as very different from, indeed complementary to, the news digests (even though both forms shared a focus on bad news). The correspondents, who showed concern about truthfulness, accuracy, and balance, seemed to have perceived their role as political and cultural analysts, not merely descriptive writers.

This chapter provides context for the study of the writings of the first U.S. foreign correspondents, explored in the next chapters. The areas of essential context include the prevalence of foreign news in selected newspapers between 1838 and 1859, and the two forms that foreign news was presented in, news digests and correspondence. The first section integrates measurement with editorial comments and other relevant information to establish how prevalent foreign news was throughout the period studied. The second section discusses differences between reprinted digests and correspondence. A third section discusses the shaping of the role of foreign correspondents, that is, how the earliest foreign correspondents conceptualized their profession and the expectations their editors and public had for them, as indicated in their writings.

THE IMPORTANCE OF FOREIGN NEWS IN MID-NINETEENTH-CENTURY NEWSPAPERS

There was a great increase in column inches of foreign news in the newspapers selected from 1838 to 1859. The amount of space devoted to foreign news, including digests, correspondence, and news briefs, more than quadrupled in the *New York Tribune* and the *Missouri Republican*; it more than doubled in the *New York Herald*, the *New Orleans Picayune*, the *Charleston Courier*, and the *Boston Transcript*. It increased only slightly in the *New York Times*, which, however, with 196 inches in 1852, had the most foreign news of any of the newspapers studied on their starting dates. The only slight decrease was found in the *Chicago Tribune*.[1]

While there was a definite increase in foreign news, the findings are mixed as to the prevalence of foreign news, that is, the amount of foreign news relative to the news hole. The amounts of foreign news were compared to the number of column inches of all news items (excluding editorials and literary matters, as well as advertisements) to determine whether the increase of foreign news was equal to, greater, or less than that of news in general. For two newspapers, the *Boston Transcript* and the *Charleston Courier*, foreign news was significantly more prevalent in 1859 than in 1838. But for the *Chicago Tribune* and the *New Orleans Picayune*, the percentage of foreign news relative to the news hole actually decreased in 1859. (A possible explanation is that by 1859 the *Tribune* was the mouthpiece of Lincoln supporters, and therefore it seems logical that it would focus on domestic issues; the *Picayune*, on the other hand, had been outstanding in reporting the news from Mexico and the Caribbean, but in 1859 the focus in foreign news was on the war in Europe.)

The *Missouri Republican*, the *New York Times*, and the *New York Tribune* had insignificant differences in percentages of foreign news (less than 1 percent) between the earliest dates of measurement and 1859. Interestingly, the *New York Herald* had a significant decrease in the percentage of foreign news relative to the news hole—from 76 percent in 1838 to 61.6 percent in 1859. However, given that in both years foreign news occupied so much *Herald* space, more than in any other paper studied, this finding suggests no lack of interest in foreign news.

The prevalence of foreign news throughout the period studied may be better assessed when these findings are integrated with editorial comments and other direct indications of how much the editors prized news from abroad. Perhaps the best statement of the importance of foreign news is revealed in a *Missouri Republican* editor's warning to readers not to be "disappointed by the want of interest in our columns for a few days" because the express mail has stopped and no news can arrive from east coast ports.[2] Indeed, editors' pride in gathering foreign news is reflected in the fact that the *New York Tribune* editor, for example, promised second editions and extras should foreign news arrive too late for the morning editions, and he dispensed with other news in order to give space to foreign news.[3] The *Herald* editor considered the arrival of foreign news momentous enough to print late extra editions at 6 P.M. with the digest just arrived from the ship.[4] He also praised his own performance in this short paragraph: "Our Canadian news, during the recent insurrections, has been invariably a day in advance of the other papers."[5] Seven years later, in the prospectus of a new supplement to the paper, he boasted: "We are now beginning to occupy the position of the only independent, comprehensive, and rational journal in this metropolis, or on this continent—our columns are filled with all kinds of news, foreign and domestic, and we uniformly endeavor, at any expense and at all hazards, to procure the earliest information on every subject, both at home and abroad."[6]

Bennett's feats, before the New York editors joined efforts to gather foreign news, caused bitter recrimination from other editors; Greeley alleged that European news from one steamer that arrived in Boston was purposely withheld from the local and New York press to be sent exclusively to Bennett at the *Herald*. In two scathing editorials, Greeley wrote that the *Tribune* too had an agent in Boston to receive the news quickly, an agent who would not have acted in the manner of the *Herald* agent, although "in fair and honorable competition his instructions as to expense are not limited."[7] A day later, Greeley reiterated that the foreign news service of the *Tribune* was "in advance of all other papers this side of Washington at least," and "yet the *Herald*, without a particle of important intelligence, had a column of gasconade about its own unparalleled enterprise and success with the Foreign news, obtained, not by expediting its receipt, but by the mean connivance of a Boston concern in keeping it back from the Boston and other New York papers."[8]

In 1859, editors expressed fury when they suspected foul play on the part of the telegraph companies. The *Boston Transcript* had a brief from St. John, New Brunswick, alleging that wire transmission had been interrupted so that speculators could get the foreign news from the just-arrived ship before the press and warning "the business public" that they were "to be made the sport of telegraph managers."[9] On the same date, this statement from the AP appeared in newspapers:

The Associated Press think it due to the public to state that the Nova Scotia Telegraph Company have, regardless of the wishes of a majority of the presses of the country and the owners of the telegraph lines west of Nova Scotia, put an end to the foreign news arrangements which have existed for the past ten years, and it is understood that the managers of the Nova Scotia line have made secret exclusive arrangements with a private party, who, there is reason to believe, will attempt to use European news for speculative purposes. For the present, therefore, the public should stand upon their guard. As soon as the Niagara's news comes to hand, it will be made public upon the bulletin boards, and until then the commercial public must be at the mercy of the Nova Scotia speculators.[10]

The *Charleston Courier* editor was no less sanguine in protesting the post office's discontinuing of the only foreign mail ship service between the southern seaboard states and Havana: "The amount of business affected by this communication was valuable, and it was of a kind that required speedy and direct communication between Havana and the cities of the South Atlantic States. . . . The travel and trade intercourse, and the best interests of Charleston, Savannah, Key West, and of South Carolina, Georgia, and a large portion of Florida, require and demand the restoration of the *Isabel*."[11] (In passing, it should be noted that the *Courier* editor seemed especially interested in business news, for not only did foreign news digests in the paper often start with the market news, but one digest was thus introduced: "The accounts are important, as showing a continued favorable state of market for American Produce."[12])

In a few instances, editors expressed doubts about the veracity of the news they received from foreign newspapers; in 1838, the *New York Herald* editor thus commented upon the news of skirmishes in Canada: "What reliance is to be placed upon this news of course we know not. There has doubtless been some movement, . . . but we doubt the accuracy of all the extracts given above."[13] On at least one occasion, an editor teased fellow editors' willingness to print fluff articles only because they came from fashionable places like France.[14] It's a statement of how important foreign news was deemed that the *New York Herald* editor would insult the editor of the *New York Courier and Enquirer*, calling him "deformed both in body and mind" and then add, as proof of the havoc his "imbecility" could wreck, "yet this genius conducts the foreign, including the *Mexican*, department, and writes the articles and makes up the news for the same."[15] But editors generally spared no praise for their own correspondents abroad. The *Charleston Courier* editor called his Central America correspondents "very attentive"; the *New York Herald* editor once thus called readers' attention to his foreign correspondence, which occupied the whole front page: "The letters of our correspondents at Paris graphically describe the imperial fêtes in honor of the triumphs of the army in Italy, and those from London, Florence, Berlin and Brussels reflect truly the state of feeling and progress of affairs."[16]

It seems evident, then, that editors throughout the period studied prized foreign news, publicizing their feats in securing it and complaining when they didn't get it quickly enough—or when it was not of good enough quality, as illustrated by this comment from the *New York Tribune* editor: "Our advices from Europe are three days later, and of the highest importance, although the latest telegram from Paris, embracing the real news, is provokingly short and unsatisfactory."[17] It seems particularly significant that in 1859 the editor of the *New York Times*, one of the editors who most sought to make his paper excel in reporting foreign news, twice expressed frustration not with competitors or with lagging telegraph lines, but with the standardized news digests provided by the telegraph. On one occasion, he wrote:

Confused as are the accounts of these great actions in the field, they are clear and coherent when compared with the political intelligence vouchsafed to us to-day by the "light-outspeeding" telegraphic current. . . . We must bear with these "fantastical tricks" in patience till the arrival of more explicit and consistent statements, congratulating ourselves meanwhile that the Atlantic Telegraph is not in operation to supply us every hour with matter for reflection equally chaotic and contradictory.[18]

Earlier that year, the *Times* editor had chided other editors for mistakenly identifying the new British minister, cautioning they could not blame "a single electrician at a seaport town" for perpetuating a *London Times* error—meaning the telegraph operator in Liverpool who brought the latest news to steamboats on their departing day.[19] The *Times* editor and his peers hailed technological innovations, so it seems likely that by 1859 these comments indicated that something more was needed from abroad than highly summarized snippets of information mostly derived from foreign newspapers. In other words, the editors might have wanted correspondence that significantly differed from the telegraphed digests.

NEWS DIGESTS AS ONE FORM OF FOREIGN NEWS

The kind of foreign news compiled and transmitted by the "single electrician" and his pre-telegraph predecessors in news digest form was studied to gain insight about the context of developments of foreign correspondence. The foreign news digests were examined in newspapers from 1838 and 1859, with particular attention to two areas: the kind of information they presented and in what order (for this indicates the editors' foreign news judgment) and the kind of tone and style of the news presentation (for this can illuminate the differences with the correspondence form).

Considering that editors continued to print the digests even as they increased their corps of foreign correspondents, the assumption here is that correspondence must have been perceived as fulfilling a purpose the digests did not and that the editors saw as necessary to full coverage of foreign affairs. As suggested by the examination of the digests and by the correspondents' own comments about their role (discussed below), it appears that by 1859 correspondence was envisioned as providing readers with context for events summarized in the digests, including cultural and political analysis. Throughout the period studied, foreign correspondence seems to have focused not only on eyewitness accounts of events, but also, and perhaps more importantly, on offering readers a personally engaging, in-depth look at the world abroad.

The format of news digests derived from foreign papers is virtually unchanged across the newspapers and periods examined, and it conforms to a routine pattern of presentation. Usually very predominantly displayed and occupying several columns or even the entire front page, a news digest is introduced by standard information about the ship that carried the mails, the length and itinerary of its Atlantic crossing, a brief summary of foreign news, and finally the digest itself. The digest is divided by country, beginning with the longest excerpts from either Great Britain (England first and then Ireland) or France, followed by the Italian states and one- or two-paragraph summaries from Spain, Germany, Switzerland, Sweden, Turkey, Syria, Greece, Russia, Poland, Egypt and French Africa, Austria, Hungary, Belgium, and the Cape of Good Hope. Less frequently, India, China, and Australia were included in these digests; separately, Latin American countries (foremost Mexico and the Caribbean islands, but also Argentina, Chile, Brazil, and Colombia) were also covered, as well as Canada. Finally, the papers examined reported the dealings of the foreign markets in great detail, usually in London, Liverpool, and Le Havre. Often, the digests would be followed by another section with longer reprints from foreign papers.[20] On days when no packet of mails arrived via ships (or later by telegraph), shorter items from these locations were interspersed with other content throughout the paper.

Clearly identifiable topics were found. Coverage in the earliest years studied focused most heavily on commerce and politics, followed by crime, natural or man-made disasters, "celebrities," and sensational, exotic news. This is hardly surprising, considering that local news consisted of the same fare. However, such a finding does seem to have significant implications for how the "world" outside the United States was constructed in these newspapers.

The predominant theme was that of armed conflict, either internal or between foreign countries, especially between colonial powers like Great Britain and France and their colonies. News of revolutions and coups was mixed with news of sensational, often trivial occurrences, especially if concerning celebrities like Victoria, queen of England, or Charles Dickens; two brief items in the *New Orleans Picayune* said that the queen had been fined for registering her son's birth late and that the writer had visited Mt. Vesuvius, the volcano outside Naples.[21] The same newspaper carried this bit of sensational (and hardly newsworthy) information: "A singular wager—at a fair in England, a fool-hardy fellow undertook, for the trifling wager of a pint of ale, to prick as many pins into the calf of his leg as would form four letters of the alphabet."[22]

One example of sensationalism from the *Herald* is illustrative: "The French papers are usually full of racy articles; the files brought by this ship are superlatively stupid. One curious fact, however, has just been developed; the municipality of Paris has sent several bakers . . . to prison, on suspicion of grinding up human bones, and mixing the dust with flour." This item was followed by the accounts of a pet fox lost in the Tuileries, Paris, a gruesome episode of attempted incest, and two suicides.[23] In the digests, early on especially, foreign facts (and rumors) were presented in such a way as to portray a strange and dangerous world outside the United States.

An 1845 *New York Herald* front page typifies the extensive digest of world news, presented quickly after the arrival of a steamship. The stacked headlines exemplify the coverage and the relative importance the editor attached to it:

Highly important! Fourteen days later from Europe. Arrival of the Hibernia. War between the Protestants and Catholics in Switzerland. Great excitement between the sects throughout Europe. Insertion of war clause in marine policies at Lloyds. A ministerial crisis in England on the Maynooth bill. Fluctuations in the cotton market. Advance in American provisions. Increase of troops in Canada. Repeal movements in Ireland. Improvement in the money market, etc. Arrival of governor Gil Davis, of Coney Island, at Paris.[24]

Such format was common across the United States. An 1845 issue of the *Missouri Republican* listed "dullness in the cotton market" and "famine in Russia"; in 1852, the *Boston Transcript* had "all quiet in France" and "Cuban prisoners all pardoned" while the *Charleston Courier* reported news of European markets and politics between France and Austria.[25] As these headlines suggest, editors seemed especially interested in foreign news of violent crises, odd occurrences, anything concerning the United States, and business. While these images of the world are reductive, the quantity and the detailed character of coverage suggest strong interest in foreign news. That editors assumed strong interest also on the part of their readers could explain the reporting of remote occurrences, including events in business and the arts. Two columns in one 1845 *New York Herald* issue, for example, are devoted to music and theater news from London, Milan, and Istanbul, among other places; a column of one 1852 *New York Tribune* issue reports on the move of a royal library in Vienna and a preview of the Paris annual exhibit of paintings.[26] An 1852 *New York Times* item from the *Mediterraneo* of Genoa, Italy, reported riots between the population of Ellera, a tiny village, and the Piedmontese police.[27]

Another subject reprinted from foreign newspapers was "industry news"—including the status of the press in other countries, or more broadly, the status of communications. Usually, this news was presented within a theme of assumed American superiority, suggesting both pride in the American press and its technological progress and a sense that the lack of similar progress in other countries was yet another sign of "uncivilized" status. This item exemplifies: "The King of one of the petty German states is opposed to anything in the shape of rail roads [*sic*]. We have known many people opposed to 'riding on a rail' who were still in favor of rail roads."[28] Other items denounced press censorship in countries like France or the slow progress of "modern" communication systems in India.[29] At least one bit of news complained about censorship of foreign correspondents in the Papal states.[30]

Little or no sensationalism was found in 1859 newspapers studied. There were strictly factual and painstakingly detailed digests, often verbatim in all the newspapers studied and, even though attribution was found to have been given only in a few cases, they were certainly prepared by The Associated Press staff.[31] For example, the *Boston Transcript*, the *New York Herald*, the *New York Tribune*, and the *New York Times* carried an identical brief from Havana: "The news is unimportant. No filibusters had been seen. Sugar was dull."[32] The following digest, from the *Charleston Courier*, shows only slight modifications from that in the New York newspapers of the same date:

The chief topic of interest from England is the reception of the President's Message, and the comments thereon. The reference in it to Cuba, Mexico and Central America, and the propositions in relation thereof, are generally unpalatable to the press. The *Times* is unusually severe in its criticism on the Message. Much surprise is manifested at the proposition to purchase Cuba, as the American Minister had already been notified that France and England were united in preventing such a transfer, even with the consent of Spain. The French troops were approaching the Swiss territory. Explanations had been demanded by Switzerland. It is rumored that France has contracted for the transportation of free negroes in large numbers into Martinique and Guadaloupe. The appeal in the Montalembert case had been heard before the Imperial Court, and the imprisonment reduced to three months, the fine been confirmed. The Portuguese Minister had been recalled from France. The U.S. war steamer Wabash was at Malta. A new company has been proposed for laying a telegraphic cable from Land's End to Halifax on a new plan.[33]

The fact that the same news appeared in Charleston and New York on the same day supports one scholar's assertion that, by 1859, The Associated Press was shaping newspaper news nationwide.[34]

The terse and yet detailed style of later digests is best exemplified by the bulletins from the seat of war in Italy in the summer of 1859: "The Allies have occupied Lonato, Castiglione, and Monte Chiaro. Napoleon had arrived at their headquarters" and "His Imperial Austrian Majesty yesterday transferred his headquarters to Villa-Franca."[35] The *New York Times* contained in their entirety the dispatches, giving city-by-city briefs, like one from Turin that read: "Yesterday the Emperor [of France] and the King [of Sardinia] quitted Brescia for the camp amid the vivas and acclamations of the populace. The Allied armies have occupied Lonato, Castiglione and Montechiaro."[36] It appears that these editors received identical digests, spelling of Montechiaro aside, and selected individually how much of them and what headlines to print; for example, one issue of the *Chicago Tribune* had fewer, but identical, European items than did the *Boston Transcript* of the same date.[37] It is noteworthy that most of the news, even about battles, was presented chronologically, with the "very latest" given at the end of the digest.[38]

In summary, then, between 1838 and 1859, the foreign news digests grew in substance and relevance, progressively leaving behind the trivial and sensationalist fare typical of the style of the earlier penny papers. The themes of conflict and political upheaval continued to remain the most prominent. Perhaps because of the new, dominating presence of The Associated Press, the 1859 digests show an unprecedented homogeneity. Initially, the AP probably did not facilitate a great change in digest content because it was still relying on European newspapers and the services of the European agencies, as discussed in the previous chapter. But it certainly streamlined the news presentation and, in order to provide its digests to papers of all political persuasions, it emphasized factual items—meaning news lacked opinion and, very often, essential background. Correspondence, as discussed in chapter 5, provided readers that kind of context and a way to understand the foreign realities described by focusing on the kinds of personal narrative and description that were absent from digests. In fact, perhaps the biggest similarity between the digests and the correspondence is that both predominantly originated in Europe, Mexico and Central America. How the correspondents sought to differentiate themselves from the "electrician at a seaport town" is the subject of the following section.

FOREIGN CORRESPONDENTS DEFINE THEIR ROLE IN A NEW OCCUPATION

"I have quite an important budget to send off to-day, although the satisfaction one feels in forwarding so full a mail bag is a good deal diminished by fear the telegraph may make it all stale before it reaches you."[39] "Gamma," the *New Orleans Picayune* Paris correspondent, suggests in this preface to his account of the battle of Magenta in the Italian war of 1859 that correspondents were aware of competition from the news digest and the need to provide their newspapers with something different, though speedy transmission of news remained of great concern.[40]

The foreign correspondents gave indication in their writings of an increasing shaping of their role and adherence to the concepts of truthfulness, accuracy, and fairness, which were developing as standards of an increasingly professional journalism. While they considered news of conflict to be the most sought after, as it was in the digests, they nevertheless tried to differentiate their reporting from the "straight" news style of the digests by also providing analyses. However, they also distanced themselves from the occasional travel writers who only focused on descriptive articles.

The findings in this section are limited to what the foreign correspondents wrote in the correspondence itself about their occupation and the expectations of their editors and public. From the references to what the writers perceived their role to be, it seems to have been understood that the correspondents' job was to analyze foreign cultures—politically and culturally—with a depth that some editors recognized was unattainable through digests and in the home offices. As the *New Orleans Picayune* editor commented in a column on "South American affairs": "The origin of the difficulties, which have now reached a crisis, is not generally understood in this country; and, indeed, *at this distance*, it is scarcely possible for us to form a correct judgment"[41] [italics added].

Some writers, in addition, extolled the importance of living in a foreign country in order to write about it with the necessary depth; for example, Bayard Taylor wrote from Japan in 1858: "A lengthened residence in the East has led me to judge of affairs, of persons, places and things, with quite a different judgment from what I would have possessed had I never been a spectator of the varied scenes which have lately transpired in that far-off world."[42] Writing in defense of full immersion in a culture, "R.W.R." of the *New York Times* argued that "some things may be learned by a pedestrian walking, eating, sleeping among the people, talking with them in their own language and gaining their confidence. And it may be of interest to your readers to know what the Tyrolese *say* of the [Italian] war, of the Government, of the future."[43] "Dean," writing from Paris about the war in Italy for the *New York Times*, emphasized: "I have been upon the ground."[44]

"Malakoff," Paris correspondent of the *New York Times*, in order to get a more accurate eyewitness account of the "manner in which the Emperor and army were received" in Paris after the Italian war, asked people stationed at different points along the parade's route "to take particular and accurate note." Incidentally, the *Times* also had another description of the event from a "special correspondent," who, however, prefaced his account by saying he did not pretend "to interfere with the regular work of your regular correspondent"—a sign that there was at least a basic understanding of the role of the professional foreign correspondent as opposed to the occasional travel writer.[45]

Several correspondents show a concern for truthfulness, or a developing concept of objectivity, which also puts them in line with the growing professionalization of journalism discussed in the previous chapter; for example, a Havana correspondent of the *New Orleans Picayune*, protesting about the confusing U.S. reports of a supposed coup in Cuba, wrote that his editors were "in duty bound, as truthful journalists" to publish his "declarations, which are not made with deliberate consideration."[46] A *New York Tribune* Paris correspondent declared himself "almost muddle[d]" by "this 'noise and confusion' of fast-rushing history," but pledged to "carry on, as well as may be, the record."[47] A *New York Herald* Paris correspondent also cautioned against the nature of his information: "I can only repeat certain *whispers* which, though they issue from a source *almost authentic*, must be received with limitations"[48] [italics added]. In a rare example of a newspaper editor praising the efforts of another, the *Chicago Tribune* editor wrote that a *New York Times* correspondent's letter about Mexican affairs could be trusted because he is "generally posted up in all that he communicates."[49] With the same pride that editors showed about "beating" the European competition, a *New York Tribune* London correspondent wrote: "I have several times called your attention to the condition of Turkey and the Russian intrigues long before the London papers had done it."[50]

The London correspondent of the *New York Tribune* showed an awareness of what today would be called "balance" by using sources from different political perspectives; he scorned the English correspondents for relying on the "gossip" of the "educated classes" in Paris, who all belonged to the same party, while he sought the opinion of the opposition too.[51] Some correspondents seem to have perceived their responsibility as providing truthful accounts, regardless of political favoritism. "Malakoff's" preface to his description of Louis Napoleon's wedding, which French papers hailed as a "brilliant affair," illustrates:

I regret, however, that the sacred rights of history demand that I should throw the smallest bucket of cold water on this appreciation. It is true that one journal, whose news-collector had some pangs of conscience in repeating the ste-reotyped phrases of the Government papers, without daring to say there was no enthusiasm, yet ventured to hint that the populace were restrained in their cries. . . . You see how difficult it is to edit a paper in Paris, and be an honest man.[52]

The correspondents' concern about accuracy might have reflected their perception of what editors expected; indeed, editors also showed concern for accuracy and balance in editing foreign news. For example, the *Chicago Tribune* editor warned that news of a French victory over Austria should be "received with some degree of allowance until the Austrian version of the affair comes to hand."[53] Similarly, the *Charleston Courier* editor ran the following note after an article by Count Camillo Cavour denouncing alleged Austrian atrocities in Italy: "This circular has received official denial from Austria."[54] Again edito-rializing about the Italian war, the *New York Herald* editor warned readers that the report by the *London Times* was biased against one party.[55]

The correspondents speculated about what kind of foreign news would be appreciated in the United States. The assumption often seems to have been that people wanted to read about crises and bad news.[56] A *Boston Transcript* correspondent seemed to complain about the pub-lic's blood-thirstiness: "[The public] has tasted blood and thinks the news of the day stupid if there are no fresh details of dreadful charges or hand to hand fights. It deems no news worthy to be read that is not red in color."[57] A *New York Herald* correspondent from Lima wrote: "I have little to communicate from this country at present. The general state of affairs is good and General Echenique continues gaining a well-merited popularity with his administration."[58] A Barbados corre-spondent for the *New York Times* wrote: "The news from the West In-dia Islands is not often of an exciting character, and I cannot promise that the present occasion forms any exception to the general rule. . . . In a journalistic point of view, the principal subject of discussion for the past some time in Barbadoes has been whether Bridgetown, the capital of the Island, shall be supplied with good water."[59]

Bayard Taylor in Hong Kong wrote of himself as being "as barren as Canning's knife-grinder," because the only topics of discussion there were European politics "you know all about," and "colonial squab-bles," which "will scarcely interest New York."[60] On the contrary, a *New Orleans Bee* correspondent found more bad news in Mexico City than he could report. Seemingly indicating that he could hardly expect

anything else, he wrote: "Since my last letter, we have had two battles—one sham and one real; another piece of treachery and some mas-
sacres and spoliations, either legal or illegal."[61] With similar apparent
condescension, a Valparaiso, Chile, correspondent for the *New York
Tribune* wrote: "Although we are shut out from the rest of the world,
still we manage to vary the monotony which generally prevails in South
America, by 'excitements' which would do honor to the 'Empire City
of the North'" (going on to write about holidays, sea storms, and earthquakes).[62]

A *New York Times* writer from Italy worried about the short attention span of his readers: "I *guess* that the protraction of the Italian Question is beginning to weary your Italian sympathy, and that all the care
and thought you have to spare from the San Juan business and the coming Presidential election is shared between the Constantinople conspiracy, the Chinese squabbles, and the Spanish flag question in
Morocco."[63] A *New York Herald* writer made fun of his peers precisely
for their focus on political speculation and conflict:

Unlike most of the Continental newspaper correspondents, who astonish their
readers in different parts of the world by their intimate knowledge of the se-
crets of State, and of the manner in which the Zurich conference is progress-
ing, and the difficulties which stand in the way of the conclusion of peace, I
profess to know nothing about the whole matter. What I do know, however, is
that it will be a melancholy day to these gentlemen when the treaty shall have
been signed, and the conference broken up, and its members returned to their
homes and the bosoms of their families, and the excitement attendant upon
the anxious waiting for them to do something shall have passed away. The
fruitful theme which has afforded material for their brains and pens to work
upon so long, will be no more of value to them, and it will be a long time before
they find in Europe another mine so rich in gems for them. I wrote you once
before that I should not trouble myself or you about wars and rumors of wars,
but should endeavor to find in the great world of Paris some less sanguinary
and more palatable food, which I might serve up to you occasionally in a letter.[64]

Suggesting that focusing on matters other than war didn't amount
to relinquishing a journalist's skills, however, the same correspondent
later in the same dispatch referred to himself as in the "capacity of
note-taker." George W. Kendall, *New Orleans Picayune* editor writing
from Paris, also seems to have clarified for his own staff that foreign correspondence should not be about trivial and odd occurrences only: "I
have filled up this letter, for the most part, with anecdotes, and items of

news circulating in the journals. You can insert it some day when the mail has failed."[65]

Several correspondents sought a clear distinction between their writings and travel letters. An Acapulco, Mexico, correspondent for the *New York Herald* wrote he was not "a very expert hand at giving sketches in foreign lands."[66] Jim Bunt, reporting from La Spezia, Italy, for the *New York Herald*, wrote: "But, as I am no romance writer, and do not profess to give you any suitable description of the place itself, I will be entirely limited to facts, and not promulgate any more than what my ideas and personal interest can answer for."[67] Bayard Taylor, writing from Hong Kong, reiterated:

I might fill a column with a description of the animated scene—of Chinese boat-women, with hair *coiffé à la* tea pot, and arms and legs eloquent of muscular exertion—of the white town, a triangle, creeping up the rugged slope of Victoria Peak—of the seemingly circular lake, five or six miles wide which constitutes the harbor, and of the novelties witnessed on every side the moment after landing. But all this has been done before, *usque ad nauseam*, and I reserve descriptions for future scenes, more fresh and thoroughly Chinese.[68]

Another correspondent joked that, in order to give a "tolerably faithful, complete, literary reproduction" of the feast at Paris for the entry of the army returning from the Italian campaign, he would need "sixty thousand lines."[69] However, many correspondents examined wrote in a beautiful, descriptive literary style; this passage, probably by Bayard Taylor himself, from the Nile Valley in Egypt, exemplifies:

The lofty shafts of the date and the vaulted foliage of the dome palm, blended in the most picturesque groupage, contrasted with the lace-like texture of the flowering mimosa, and the cloudy boughs of a kind of gray cypress. The turf under the trees was soft and green, and between the slim trunks we looked over the plains, to the Libyan Mountains—a long chain of rosy lights and violet shadows.[70]

Despite this literary orientation, it was in 1859 correspondence, not in the telegraphic digests, that an instance of breaking the rule of chronological presentation was found, although accompanied by the correspondent's apology: "Let me begin a very imperfect attempt to serve up the two great Feasts of Sunday and Monday and their accessories, in defiance of the laws of the table and chronology, with the best things first and with the decree published only a few hours ago."[71]

In summary, findings about context of developing foreign correspondence suggest that foreign news was highly prized by editors
throughout the period studied, and that correspondents understood
their occupation as providing something that the factual, terse snippets
of information in the news digests could not offer. It appears that foreign correspondents went abroad intent on reporting foreign cultures
accurately (if with a penchant for emphasizing conflict in their reports)
and analytically. The perceptions of the "world" in the culture receiving
their correspondence may be found in the images of foreign cultures in
editorials and foreign policy congressional records, discussed in the
next chapter.

NOTES

1. The *New York Times* had 196 inches of foreign news in 1852, or 27.4
percent of the news hole; it had 207.5 inches in 1859, or 26.1 percent. The
Boston Transcript had 45 inches of foreign news in 1838, or 32.6 percent of
the news hole; it had 90 inches in 1859, or 37.6 percent. The *Missouri Republican* had 11.5 inches of foreign news in 1838, or 26.8 percent; it had at
least 77 inches in 1859 (difficult to estimate exactly because of the poor quality of the extant copies), or 26.7 percent. The *Chicago Tribune* had 38.5
inches of foreign news in 1853, or 25 percent of the news hole; it had 32.5
inches in 1859, or 12.4 percent. The *Charleston Courier* had 28 inches of
foreign news in 1838, or 16.5 percent of the news hole; it had 81.5 inches in
1859, or 21.8 percent. The *New Orleans Picayune* had 59.5 inches of foreign
news in 1838, or 55.1 percent of the news hole; it had 166.5 inches in 1859,
or 36.7 percent. The *New York Tribune* had 33.5 inches of foreign news in
1845, or 28.8 percent of the news hole; it had 165 inches in 1859, or 27.3
percent. The *New York Herald* had 165 inches of foreign news in 1838, or
76 percent of the news hole; it had 386.5 inches in 1859, or 61.6 percent.

2. *Missouri Republican*, May 3, 1838, p. 2.

3. *New York Tribune*, December 5 and 6, 1845, p. 2; July 21, 1845,
p. 2: "We are obliged to lay over our Washington letter—a rather rich one,
by the way—by the pressure of Fire [in New York] and Foreign News." In
1859, the *Boston Transcript* revealed the same attitude: "We present below as
many extracts from the English papers, brought by the latest steamers, as our
limit will permit," July 8, p. 1.

4. *New York Herald*, July 3, 1845. The editor must have been rushing
to get the foreign news out, for there is a very obvious typographical error in
a front page headline, which reads "Francf and Texas."

5. *New York Herald*, December 8, 1838, p. 2.

6. *New York Herald*, May 9, 1845, p. 2.

7. *New York Tribune*, December 8, 1845, p. 2.

8. *New York Tribune*, December 9, 1845, p. 2.

9. *Boston Transcript*, May 5, 1859, p. 2, and May 6, 1859, p. 2.

10. Printed on May 5, 1859, on p. 4 of the *Chicago Tribune*, the *New York Tribune*, and the *New York Herald*.

11. *Charleston Courier*, September 1, 1859, p. 2.

12. *Charleston Courier*, May 7, 1852, p. 2.

13. *New York Herald*, December 13, 1838, p. 2; also, *Missouri Republican*, January 10, 1845, p. 2, carries a story from Mexico "not without some doubt of its genuineness."

14. On the "news" that French noblewomen lusted after Prince Albert of England: "We were about to say something harsh at the appearance of such articles as the above, without a word of rebuke or disapprobation, in American journals, but we know how easily paragraphs sometimes slip into daily papers, and how difficult it is, in a season when French literature and French morals are in fashion, utterly to avoid them. So let it pass"; *New York Tribune*, July 26, 1845, p. 2.

15. *New York Herald*, July 28, 1838, p. 2.

16. *Charleston Courier*, January 3, 1852, p. 2; *New York Herald*, September 2, 1859, p. 4.

17. *New York Tribune*, July 7, 1859, p. 4.

18. *New York Times*, July 7, 1859, p. 4.

19. *New York Times*, January 6, 1859, p. 4.

20. For example, "Additional European News by the City of Washington [boat]: . . . Much of her news had been telegraphed, but we extract from our European papers many additional items of interest," *Charleston Courier*, September 2, 1859, p. 1. Also, on p. 2 of the *New Orleans Picayune* of the same date: "We gave a pretty full telegraphic synopsis of the European news brought by the steamship Etna. . . . In the more full dispatches in the New York papers, of the 27th ult., we find no details of interest not heretofore given in a condensed shape."

21. *New Orleans Picayune*, January 3, 1845, p. 2 and May 1, 1845, p. 2.

22. *New Orleans Picayune*, May 11, 1838.

23. *New York Herald*, December 12, 1838, p. 2.

24. *New York Herald*, May 8, 1845.

25. *Missouri Republican*, November 6, 1845, p. 3; *Boston Transcript*, January 2, 1852, p. 2; *Charleston Courier*, January 3, 1852, p. 2.

26. *New York Herald*, September 5, 1845, p. 2 (for example, "[Giacomo] Puccini was ill at his residence at Lucca [Italy]"); *New York Tribune*, March 5, 1852, p. 7.

27. *New York Times*, July 26, 1852, p. 1. A similarly very localized item of business news appeared in the *New York Herald*'s May 7, 1852, issue (p. 2): "The Milan Gazette announces that the duty on wine imported from Piedmont into Lombardy had been diminished, and coal and various other

articles admitted free of duty, in execution of the commercial treaty with Sardinia."

28. *New Orleans Picayune*, January 5, 1838, p. 2.

29. "The new crusade against the press in France continued to be pushed with vigor," *New Orleans Picayune*, September 6, 1838, p. 2; "miserable parsimony" delayed the development of the electric telegraph in India, according to the *Ceylon Journal*, in the *New York Herald*, November 4, 1852, p. 3. Also, *New Orleans Picayune*, March 4, 1852, p. 2; *New York Tribune*, January 2, 1852, p. 3.

30. "It is not easy to get authentic intelligence from Rome, Cardinal Antonelli having declared war upon the foreign correspondents, stopped their letters and threatened to turn them out of the city," from the *London News*, reprinted in the *Charleston Courier*, January 7, 1859, p. 2.

31. The foreign news digest printed on page 1 of the May 6, 1859 issue of the *Charleston Courier* is prefaced by the note: "From the Ass. Press" and datelined Halifax. In the July 7, 1859, issues of the *Boston Transcript* and the *New York Tribune*, the foreign news digests are prefaced by this note: "Steamship Vigo was intercepted off Cape Race [Newfoundland] at 3 o'clock this A.M., by the news boat of the Associated Press, and her news dispatches obtained." "Associated Press" is also printed at the end of a brief, market news digest on the front page of the January 6, 1859, issue of the *New Orleans Picayune*.

32. May 5, 1859, *Boston Transcript*, p. 1; *New York Herald*, p. 4; New York Tribune, p. 4; *New York Times*, p. 1.

33. *Charleston Courier*, January 6, 1859, p. 1.

34. Menahem Blondheim, *News Over the Wires* (Cambridge, Mass.: Harvard University Press, 1994): 195.

35. *Charleston Courier*, July 7, 1859, p. 1.

36. *New York Times*, July 8, 1859, p. 1.

37. January 6, 1859, *Chicago Tribune*, p. 1 and *Boston Transcript*, p. 4.

38. *New York Tribune*, July 7, 1859, p. 5.

39. *New Orleans Picayune*, July 7, 1859, p. 1.

40. A London correspondent for the *New York Herald* wrote, "but let me ask what concerns news more than the mode of its transit? Next to the privilege of being able to speak out or write out at all, as they cannot do in despotic countries, comes the question of rapid, frequent and punctual dispatch and delivery of news"; *New York Herald*, September 2, 1859, p. 1.

41. *New Orleans Picayune*, January 1, 1852, p. 1.

42. Correspondence of the *New York Tribune*, reprinted in the *Boston Transcript*, January 6, 1859, p. 1. A *New York Times* correspondent from Italy thus validated his authority in speculating about the future of the country: "I have watched and lived in Italian affairs so long"; *New York Times*, November 3, 1859, p. 2.

43. *New York Times*, November 4, 1859, p. 2.

44. *New York Times*, July 8, 1859, p. 1.

45. *New York Times*, September 1, 1859, p. 1; September 2, 1859, p. 1.

46. *New Orleans Picayune*, May 6, 1859, p. 1.

47. *New York Tribune*, July 15, 1859, p. 5.

48. *New York Herald*, January 6, 1859, p. 1.

49. *Chicago Tribune*, September 8, 1853, p. 2.

50. *New York Tribune*, November 5, 1852, p. 7; signed A.F.C.

51. *New York Tribune*, July 8, 1859, p. 5.

52. *New York Times*, March 3, 1859, p. 2.

53. *Chicago Tribune*, July 7, 1859, p. 1.

54. *Charleston Courier*, July 8, 1859, p. 1.

55. *New York Herald*, March 3, 1859, p. 4. The *Herald* also ran a correction from its Acapulco correspondent saying that nobody had died aboard a vessel, as the newspaper had reported; November 3, 1859, p. 5.

56. "The momentous events enacting in Europe obtain a consideration rarely bestowed upon distant interests in this country," wrote the *Boston Transcript* editor of the 1859 Italian war; June 28, 1859.

57. *Boston Transcript*, July 8, 1859, p. 2.

58. *New York Herald*, January 8, 1852, p. 3. Also, "In matter of correspondence, I can't say a great deal. Italy seems to be quiet. Nothing of political consequence is transacting," *New York Herald*, November 5, 1852, p. 2.

59. *New York Times*, March 4, 1859, p. 1. The *New York Times* editor seemed to hold the same news judgment, for an item from Honduras began, "there is no news of importance. The country remained tranquil, and there is nothing of a political character to report"; January 7, 1859, p. 5.

60. *New York Tribune*, September 1, 1859, p. 6.

61. Reprinted in the *New York Times*, January 6, 1859, p. 2. Similarly, the editor of the *New York Herald* commented on the news from Lima, Peru: "As usual revolutions were the order of the day"; *New York Herald*, January 2, 1845, p. 1.

62. *New York Tribune*, May 6, 1852, p. 4.

63. *New York Times*, November 3, 1859, p. 2.

64. *New York Herald*, November 3, 1859, p. 2.

65. In his letter, he wrote about Americans he ran into in Paris ("one certainly meets them at every turn and corner"); the "amusing story" of an Englishman traveling in Vienna; the divorce of a prima donna of the Lyons theater; a "singular suicide"; and the misadventures of a "wealthy heiress" from Germany; *New Orleans Picayune*, March 5, 1852, p. 2.

66. *New York Herald*, November 3, 1859, p. 5.

67. *New York Herald*, November 5, 1852, p. 2.

68. *New York Tribune*, September 1, 1859, p. 6.

69. *New York Tribune*, September 2, 1859, p. 6.

70. *New York Tribune*, March 4, 1852, p. 6.

71. *New York Tribune*, September 2, 1859, p. 6.

CHAPTER 4

IMAGES OF THE "WORLD" IN MID-NINETEENTH-CENTURY U.S. CULTURE

Editorials and texts of congressional debates suggest that, between 1838 and 1859, the context for an understanding of foreign realities in the United States focused on American superiority and some interpretation of a sense of the country's mission to lead the rest of the world. The world was portrayed in a somewhat ambivalent fashion, as both in need to acknowledge the United States' leading role and to fulfill its own promise by trying to elevate itself to the American standard.

CONSTRUCTIONS OF THE "WORLD" IN EDITORIALS

This section examines the discursive constructions of the "world" in the editorials dealing exclusively with foreign affairs in selected newspapers. Editorial comments interspersed with the news were also read, as were the daily editorials found in the New York papers, summarizing and explaining the significance of the news of the day. Lengthy quotations are used here to facilitate understanding of the constructions. Even though most editorials were found in the New York papers, the constructions recurred in papers read from the South and the West. Virtually unanimously, the editorials read suggest a belief in the American mission or in the United States as destined to a superior position among nations, and in the assumption that other nations could only benefit from American intervention or at least influence. Such a construction of the "world" reveals an imperialistic tendency, a belief in providential mission and manifest destiny. Those same themes as found in foreign policy are discussed in the next section.

Of all possible positions, that of an independent journalist is the most trying which any man of sense and character can fill. . . . As a matter of private ease and comfort nothing can be more agreeable than the attitude of devoted partisanship. . . . But we also need a really impartial Press, committed to no special organization—social, commercial, or political—independent of all factions, and devoted entirely to the task of examining each public question as it arises, upon its merits alone.[1]

With those words, the *New York Times* editor defended his method of dealing with foreign matters after having been attacked for praising the British foreign minister. In fact, he wrote that, since the *Times* had been attacked from both sides on international questions, its course was independent—an argument similar to today's journalists' contention that, if they are judged partial by both liberals and conservatives, they must indeed be objective.

Significant as that *Times* editorial is, it is the single exception found among the blatantly partisan editorializing about foreign matters. A statement from the *New York Herald* best symbolizes the editors' sentiment found throughout the 1838–1859 period—the United States was "in the high position of leader and feeder of the civilized world."[2]

Several constructions in the editorials reveal these themes, exemplifying a discourse of American superiority. One construction, found especially in the *New York Herald*, suggests that other countries need to be reminded of how powerful the United States is and learn to honor the American role in world history. Another construction, which suggests that the world is violent, rife with conflict, and a possible threat to the American people and their interests led to the most aggressive construction: It seemed aimed at rallying the American public and officials to a position of leadership and intervention because other countries were constructed as so inherently barbaric and/or poorly governed that American intervention was not only justified, but a moral imperative.

Editorials suggest that editors were especially concerned with tying foreign affairs to domestic topics and thus promulgating their views on the latter, especially on such topics as slavery, territories, and pro-English or pro-French factions. Editors seemed to have defined audience interest in foreign affairs primarily as they involved American interests: "There is nothing in relation to the United States in any of the papers," the *New York Herald* editor complained in an 1845 editorial. From the same newspaper: "[News from Europe] was looked for with much anxiety, because people expected to hear new developments of the sentiments of the British government, in relation to Oregon, Texas, and other matters."[3]

The *New Orleans Picayune* and the *New York Herald* editorials especially show the construction of foreign countries as in need of reckoning with the United States. In a commentary on a "very clever" *London Times* article about the subjugation of India, the *New Orleans Picayune* editor wrote in alarmist tones: "The enslaving of a hundred millions of people affords a neat subject for a joke. The Times would be immensely facetious if all America were reduced as India has been."[4] The following passage about an American fleet sailing for Japan illustrates the same attitude:

[The ships] will present a very imposing array of force to the Japanese, upon whom some such exhibition is necessary to give an idea of the power of the United States. In that section of country America is an unknown region, holding an obscure place in the corner of the map upon which Japan and China are preeminent central Empires. Some display of force beyond that of an ordinary mercantile enterprise is required to convince these people that the Americans are a people fit to be dealt with as a nation.[5]

Bennett's commentary on the Oregon question epitomizes this attitude: "John Bull [the British] at last is frightened at Brother Jonathan [the American]. Good."[6] In fact, Bennett complained that the U.S. government was not assuming an international leadership becoming to its stature:

[W]ith vacillation on one side and inaction on the other, on many of the vital questions of our national progress and international intercourse, the position of every American Minister abroad—in Europe and out of it—has been lowered in an immense degree; and it is far below that which corresponds to our industrial and commercial importance, our intellectual development, our territorial extent, and the vast future which the world now concedes to us.[7]

Bennett lamented the lack of respect other countries showed for the United States' foreign policy aims; to wit, "There is less swaggering bombast and insolent bravado, and a tolerable sprinkling of moderation and common sense in the recent articles of the London press on American affairs."[8] He wrote that the "democratic expansion" between "our Atlantic and Pacific empires," with which the United States "should have written the destiny" of the Caribbean, was threatened by European powers; while "no Power has yet been able to prevent the continued growth in power, influence and impudence of the United States," a more aggressive policy was needed to "vindicate the honor of the country."[9] During the 1859 Italian war, Bennett similarly wrote that the belligerent powers must "respect our just rights" to sea trade (ever prone to agitate for a more active U.S. role on the international stage, he continued, "and to make these to be respected we must be ready to defend them. Our navy will be called into the most active service"), and then the United States can take "a leadership among the nations in humanizing the art of war."[10]

The usually moderate *New York Times* editor also wrote that the "outrages" against Americans in Acapulco deserved "measures more palpable" from the U.S. government:

American citizens have time and again been deprived of their property, liberty, and even life, at Acapulco, either by order of the local authorities, or under their eye and without their interference. Finding that such agreeable amusements could be indulged in with impunity so long as a "cursed Yankee" was the victim of their sport, the excitement of the game passed away with its novelty; and now they transfer their manifestations of hate to the only representative of our Government in their midst![11]

The *Times* editor, arguing for the annexation of Canada, wrote similarly in 1852 of the relationship between the United States and the rest of the world, which is indicative of how pervasive this construction was. The editor wrote:

Acquisitiveness stands out on the national cranium. . . . Let our British friends at the North make us unpleasantly sensible of their existence . . . and it is no telling how soon we shall swallow them, headland and inland, lake, river and town. We speak more in sorrow than arrogance. We shall have to do it; that is all. . . . Insults fall upon us thicker and faster. Our ships sail up and down the Mediterranean, with a white flag at the mast head, for fear of offending the President of France. Feeble, tottering Spain, brings us to her decrepit feet, to beg the liberty of our citizens, whose confinement was a gross act of contumely. Mexico [takes] courage from the general example. . . . The authorities of Greece, with similar contempt for the dignity of our Government, condemn and fine our agent at Athens. England, after practically treating the Clayton treaty as a nullity, by repeated violations of it, and insults to our flag, has the audacity to send an agent to Washington. . . . And how far must we have sunk in the scale of dignity and respectability![12]

A related construction, with further implications for aggressive foreign policy, suggests that foreign countries are naturally rich, but their peoples are so violent and/or poorly governed that they are inherently inferior to the United States. Moreover, they can represent a threat to Americans. Bennett wrote in 1838, for example: "Mexico [is] one of the most splendid places on earth, and brutality and villany of the Mexican men have made it one of the most miserable places for the residence of a Christian that can be found upon the face of the earth [since] they murder, rob, rape and torture innocent aliens."[13] Seven years later, Bennett wrote of Haiti: "It appears that Hayti [*sic*] cannot remain quiet. With elements enough to become a comparatively wealthy Republic, she is rapidly going to ruin."[14]

A statement in the same newspaper in 1852 shows similar judgments about European countries: "Neither France, Italy, Spain, or Southern Germany, have any real conception of true liberty. All they desire is a moral and social freedom; but they do not comprehend, or, knowing, disregard religious and political liberty. . . . Under this view, there is no hope for the establishment of liberal republican institutions in Europe, such as we enjoy in the United States. . . . The idea is mere moonshine, without palpable form or shape."[15] In 1859, the *Chicago Tribune* editor wrote that the citizens of the Papal states in central Italy were "misgoverned to an extent of which Americans can form but a faint concept" and, in 1853, he thus described American interest in Latin America: "The condition of the Southern Continent is daily becoming a matter of more interest to the United States. . . . The keen Yankee keels [are] cutting [the Amazon's] mammoth branches, and frightening the wild men of those immense unexplored regions, with their hurrahs for Washington and Liberty."[16]

The step is short from these constructions, emphasizing foreign countries as barbaric and potentially threatening, to constructions of the "world" as awaiting redeeming American intervention, either in the form of annexation or enlightening influence at the very least. Editorializing in 1845 about Mexico, Kendall epitomized this construction: "We must conquer it, free it, unite it with us; give it the benefit of our freedom, our intelligence, our energy; guide and elevate it by American mind."[17] Bennett wasn't coy about his views of Mexico either; in an 1852 editorial entitled "Another crisis—what is to be done?" he wrote: "In short, the crisis is rapidly approaching in Mexico, when we shall be called upon to decide whether that vast republic, with its vast and varied and undeveloped resources of wealth, commerce, greatness and happiness, shall be turned over as a protectorate or colony of

Great Britain, or become an integral portion of the territories of these United States."[18]

Regarding Cuba, the *New Orleans Picayune* editor reiterated in 1859 that it is "a chimera of the imagination" to expect change "without some external aid, and which only a powerful government can give."[19] Again about Cuba, the *New York Times* editor argued that American citizens had been suffering from the island's regime and, most significantly, that Cuba wasn't as useful to its northern neighbor as it could justly be expected to be: "Our Commerce isn't enjoying all we have a right to claim or expect of Cuba. . . . We deem it anything but safe to leave the avenue from our Atlantic to our Gulf and Pacific States in the control of a power, of whose petulance and insolence we have had ample experience"; as a disclaimer, the editor then added: "nor do we at any time insist upon the value of Cuba to this country as an argument for recourse to violent methods."[20]

Two 1859 editorials from the same newspaper, arguing in favor of American intervention in Mexico, best exemplify this construction; the construction seems based on assumptions that the Mexicans were incapable of self-government, that they would benefit from U.S. influence and, perhaps most importantly, they were so close to the United States that their problems could not be ignored (or, put another way, the concept is that proximity qualifies the American sense of providential mission to provide an example to other countries). The editor wrote:

It may be—and we fear it is—that the Mexicans are unfit for any other kind of native rule [than colonialism]; such a system is entirely unfitted for this vicinity, and cannot exist so near the United States. . . . The fact is, that few people in Europe—and least of all, the French—understand Republicanism. . . . But we do not think that Mexico should be pronounced totally incapable of profiting by the example of the United States until she shall have had an opportunity of living under a real Republic. . . . What is now wanted is, that the United States should follow [recognition of Juarez's government] up by substantial support, in order that the Liberal and Constitutional President of the Mexican Republic may hold his ground till the people come round to him, which they will do the moment they understand our friendship can be relied on. . . . Now is the time for us to establish an influence which shall be better to us than annexation, and to Mexico than any event she has witnessed in the last one hundred years. . . . If Mexico were as capable of self-government as our neighbor to the North, we would have no occasion to meddle with her. If she were located on the other side of the round world, there would be no call for even interference. But she is at our door: her disorders and turmoils visit their effects upon us; our citizens suffer from her bad government; we cannot let her alone with safety. Now is the time for beneficial intervention. Shall we have it?[21]

In a few cases, editors did praise (albeit condescendingly) some elements of other countries. Some suggested that the people in those countries indeed were aware of their "wretched" condition; for example, the editor of the *Boston Transcript* wrote that Italians showed "a moderation and discretion worthy of the highest praise," leading him to think that "there is hope for any race" and that they "have made rapid strides toward that self-restraint necessary for the assertion of national independence." He went on to state that "in Central Italy, though suddenly deprived of its normal rule, and utterly destitute of any organized means of expression, there is less violence and less outrage than an ordinary borough election would present in England."[22] While acknowledging that American treatment of the Chinese in California was "a little rough," the same editor congratulated "John Chinaman" on taking the "initiatory steps of civilization" by submitting to "a gentle force ... converting you into a neighbor and annexing, commercially and morally, your Flowery kingdom to Christendom."[23]

Three editorials were found that opposed territorial conquest of Mexico. Only one seemed to be motivated by respect for the native people: The *New York Tribune* editor wrote that the administration was intent on "gnawing and nibbling at poor Mexico" only because the purchase of Cuba was delayed and it perceived the need to "stay the public stomach."[24] The *New York Times* editor, whose views on "Mexican redemption" were noted above, rejoiced in 1859 that the "Washington peddlers have ceased to make their miserable bids for slices of Mexican territory."[25] The *Chicago Tribune* editor also opposed annexation, but because "the country has enough of the half-civilized element now ... without going among the semi-barbarians of Mexico for more." Writing in 1859, he continued:

The argument that without our interference, the Mexicans will destroy each other in their interminable wars, is worthless. The Mexicans are a free people; and if they choose to fight, ours is not the responsibility or the loss. It is a dangerous doctrine that we are the guardians of all our neighbors; and that we must be armed mediators in their endless and numberless quarrels. They are acting out their religion and civilization, as we are acting out ours. If that leads them to mutual and unsparing destruction, good will by and by come out of the evil; Mr. Buchanan and the American Congress may not presume to interfere with the ordinations of Providence.... It will be thought that we are willing that the Mexicans should fight. So we are, to their heart's content. When they have depopulated the country by their military and judicial murders, there will then be room and opportunity for the emigration of men and women of Anglo-Saxon and pure Saxon blood, to whom all modern civilization is due.[26]

That editorial indicates, aside from racism, a theme of isolationism that coexisted with the proto-imperialist discourse. As discussed later in this chapter, the enthusiasm "to conquer and elevate" the rest of the world was constrained by the fear that involvement in foreign affairs might contaminate the American spirit. Perhaps because of this fear, and perhaps because of the lack of proximity,[27] no mention was found of intervention in European affairs during the 1859 war.

But the editors did take sides; they were particularly unforgiving in their condemnation of Austria, described as a tyrannical state with a "despotic and detestable cause" of trampling Italian independence.[28] In a sarcastic comment about an Austrian defeat, the *Boston Transcript* editor wrote: "So endeth the second lesson of Austrian courage and ability when matched against French military skill, foresight and energy"; the *Chicago Tribune* editor, commenting upon the same Austrian loss, added: "We are sorry that we cannot add that she is politically blotted out from among the governments of the earth."[29] The *New York Tribune* editor wrote that he could not decide whether Austria was worse than France, which fought with the Italians but was guided by another despot, Napoleon; however, he rejoiced that "Revolution once more stalks forth over Europe."[30] On the contrary, the *New York Herald* editor expressed appreciation for Napoleon's presence, for it would "prevent this sweeping revolution, and the anarchy consequent upon it"; the editor was particularly weary of Italian popular leader Giuseppe Mazzini, whom he called "the red revolutionist and the assassin."[31]

While they did not recommend U.S. intervention, several editorials about the 1859 war suggest an interesting corollary to the construction of the civilizing American role in the world. Several editors wrote about the conflict in terms of "superpowers" (especially Russia and Germany) that would have the decisive role in the destiny of smaller countries. The *Boston Transcript* editor said that Russia's position would be "all important" as it might be attracted into the fray by "schemes of aggrandizement."[32] The *New Orleans Picayune* editor wrote that English antiwar sentiment was justified by the danger of "breaking up by war the territorial apportionment of the great Empires of the Continent."[33] Bennett stated that the outcome of the war would "depend upon the ranging of nations."[34] Thus, even when the American nation was not directly involved, the editors seem to have constructed foreign events as a rather arbitrary arrangement by the large colonial powers.[35]

As mentioned above, not all editorials on foreign affairs were unsympathetic to foreign peoples or solely concerned with American implications. Bennett wrote in 1852: "We are sorry to learn that the cholera is raging with the most frightful malignity in Russia and Poland"; Greeley, in 1852 and again in 1859, ran detailed, clearly supportive editorials on the labor movement in England.[36]

Nevertheless, by far the dominant construction in editorials on foreign affairs might have led readers to believe the world was on the brink of crisis and incapable of resolving its own problems without American enlightenment. American superiority to the rest of the world was a tenet in virtually all editorials read. Some discursive constructions imply a world that needs to reckon with the leading role of the United States, a world that is so conflict-ridden that little hope can be entertained of its redemption without intervention, and that intervention then becomes morally justified. These constructions fit the broader discourse of a providential American mission, and they seem a logical precursor of, or they laid a foundation for, full-blown imperialism by century's end. Moreover, these constructions parallel trends in American foreign policy of the time, which are discussed below.

CONSTRUCTIONS OF THE "WORLD" IN FOREIGN POLICY DEBATES

Imbued as they are with the doctrine of Manifest Destiny, congressional debates on foreign affairs differ from editorials only in the greater extent policymakers emphasized the threat represented by the foreign powers and the need for the United States to prove its providential leading role.

Constructions of the "world" were identified in congressional discussion of two foreign policy matters—the annexation of Texas (for the last three months before it was approved in March 1845) and governmental aid for the first laying of the Atlantic cable in 1857.[37] There was no intention to establish whether the constructions in the press influenced foreign policy discussions, or the other way around, nor to show the effect of either on the public. In fact, studies of media influence upon policymakers, and vice versa, come to opposite conclusions. With the overarching question of the quantity and quality of information Americans receive from the media about foreign affairs,[38] literature is divided in two branches, both examining only twentieth-century examples. Some argue that the press affects foreign policy, or at least policymakers perceive it to have a significant role; others believe that policymakers affect the press.[39] One scholar refutes both positions, arguing that the media and the foreign policy establishment are one; however, he also argues that foreign correspondents are more critical in covering foreign policy than are their colleagues in Washington.[40]

While this section doesn't purport to compare constructions in foreign correspondence and editorials with constructions in foreign policy discussions, similarities are noted to emphasize the evidence of the pervasiveness of certain constructions. What this section seeks, rather, is to examine the foreign policy trends and some of the ways the "world" was talked about by officials in Washington during the period studied. This information also is a part of the context necessary for the discussion of the development of foreign correspondence and of images of the "world" in America at the time.

Two studies of ideology in American foreign policy throughout the country's history found a constant trend—a sense of mission mixed with self-righteousness. Whitcomb argues that a myth of superiority is ingrained in the American approach to foreign affairs. This should not be confused with self-interest, he asserts, but seen rather as a concept of mission; he claims that Americans believe they are unique in the world, but they also believe that other countries are capable of rising to the "American level" (hence the mission).[41] Hunt, who emphasizes racial and ethnic hierarchies in the ideology of foreign policymaking, adds that there is a lack of self-consciousness about this ideology and that Americans have also been troubled by the problem of reconciling liberty at home with an assertive presence in the world's affairs.[42] The ideology of mission allowed the nation to establish its social and political worth to the extent that it seemed the nation should get involved in international affairs[43]—a corollary to the assumption that identifying the other involves defining the self.

The construction of the United States' role in the world as an elevating mission has been noted in the editorials discussed above. During the period studied, especially through the 1840s, but also in the 1850s, this role was most strongly revealed in the Manifest Destiny doctrine. "'Manifest Destiny' was the ultimate expression of the Americans' most vigorous hopes for raising the rest of the world to their own level," according to historian Rush Welter.[44] From this perspective, the Manifest Destiny doctrine was more than a Providence-inspired excuse for aggressive territorial expansion and for the widely held belief that foreign countries, especially on the American continent, could be truly free only if conquered by the United States. Indeed, as Welter convincingly points out, idealism had a part in American expansionist policies. Even though Americans were "complacent" about the role history seemed to have assigned to them and blissfully indifferent to the rights of other nations, they considered their efforts a "heroic step toward righting wrongs from which the rest of the world suffered"; since they were going about the work of spreading the realization of liberty and progress, they seem to have assumed that liberal-minded people everywhere would not object.[45]

Throughout the period under study, territorial expansion was the utmost concern in foreign policy making, accompanied by a presumed need to establish the United States' position in the eyes of the world's powers, especially England. Until the early 1840s, the main diplomatic challenges for U.S. foreign policymakers were border squabbles with Canada, which was agitating for independence from British rule.[46] By 1844, two territories became the crucial points of contention with the British, and also with France, Spain, and Mexico—Oregon and Texas. The issues of annexation dominated the presidential campaign and contributed to James Polk's election. During the fight over Oregon, a New York editor used the phrase "manifest destiny," a concept used by another editor two decades earlier. Texas was annexed in March 1845, and Mexico broke diplomatic relations with the United States. In April 1846, the two countries engaged in war, which ended two years later with the Treaty of Guadalupe Hidalgo; Mexico lost nearly half of its territory, including California, to the United States.

In the 1850s, internal politics, especially growing sectionalism, overshadowed foreign affairs. The movement for annexation, though, did not disappear; in fact, aggressive foreign policy might have become even more attractive to combat sectional antagonism.[47] It recurred in the quest for the control of maritime routes in Central America and the efforts to purchase Cuba. Further, even if without practical consequences, sympathy for the European revolutions around 1848 captivated American public opinion. And in the 1850s the United States was involved with opening trade with China, and led the way in opening trade with Japan.

Some scholars have argued that economic growth was the driving force behind the era's expansionism, as the United States grew as a power in world trade and eventually into an imperialistic force.[48] (Several scholars also see in the Manifest Destiny doctrine, and in the fear of British expansion threatening such destiny, the earliest roots of the American imperialism of the late 1890s.)[49] But the explanation of a national myth of mission is more convincing than is the theory of economic determinism. Frederick Merk, who exhaustively treated the myth in his 1963 book, *Manifest Destiny*, found in the ideology of Manifest Destiny a belief in self-realization, that is, other countries that benefited by American intervention could truly exploit their resources and undergo regeneration.[50] This construction was found in editorials of the time, as discussed above. Merk argued that the penny press, because of its sensationalism, espoused the Manifest Destiny doctrine and helped make it a national conviction—virtually unchallenged, if one understands the doctrine to be expressed not only in the issue of annexation but also in the concept that the United States had a mission as "the light" to the world.[51]

The annexation of Texas made the Manifest Destiny doctrine a national ideology, joining continentalism with the perceived need to stave off European threats to North American freedom.[52] The U.S. Senate and the House of Representatives passed a resolution to discuss jointly the matter on January 3, 1845; the House approved annexation on January 25, while the Senate approved it on February 27. Representative C.J. Ingersoll, chairman of the Committee on Foreign Affairs, spoke first on January 3 and disposed of the question of the right of annexation by claiming: "The territorial limits are marked in the configuration of this continent by an Almighty hand."[53]

What's interesting here, as noted, is the broader discussion involving not only Texas, but the international perspective to the proposed annexation. One scholar's assertion that Texas, Oregon, and the Mexican war made up a "truly international question," which helped propel the United States onto the world's stage,[54] was substantiated to a remarkable degree by the importance congressmen attached to this angle. Ingersoll turned to it in his opening speech, and his statements, an overview of American foreign policy at the time, deserve quoting at length:

Having thus disposed of the policy and right to reannex Texas, let us consider what other nations have to say to it—Mexico, Great Britain, France and the rest of the world; for we are amenable to Russia, Austria, Prussia, Spain, Naples, Holland, Belgium; and why not to Brazil, Buenos Ayres, Chili [*sic*] and Venezuela, as to Great Britain, the most pragmatic among the protestants against our action. As there was a time when the United States cultivated entire segregation from European connection, so now it is our policy to prevent foreign interference in our affairs. Our growth, numerous treaties and extensive intercourse with nearly all the world,—have established the United States in the family of nations. The administration endeavored to arrange an American alliance to comprehend this hemisphere. While peace and forbearance are still our interests, it is plain that, by commerce and naval forces in every sea, embassies in every country, and *irresistible tendencies, we are, though not a meddling, yet a moving people.* [italics added]

Such terminology reflects the construction observed, especially in Bennett's editorials, that the rest of the world needed to reckon with the United States. Ingersoll insisted that annexation was threatened by "the menaces of Mexico and the machinations of other powers," while Senator William Allen, of Ohio, argued that "The object of the federal government was to unite Massachusetts and Louisiana and Texas in one common country against influences from without. The object of its framers was to make a common struggle against the despots of Europe." Senator George McDuffie, of South Carolina, in the closing days of the debate, harped that if the United States "lost" Texas, the country "would be the jest and laughing stock of Europe."[55]

This suggests, interestingly, that the concept of the Manifest Destiny doctrine (America's mission to the world) contained an ambivalence in the sense that the "superior" United States needed to secure the respect of international powers. This is implied also in Ingersoll's argument that the "recovery of Texas" was supported by Americans also because of "a deep-seated, well-nigh-universal sentiment of national independence, which will not tolerate European interference with our affairs, our borders, our institutions, our unquestionable rights." Representative John Weller, of Ohio, took the argument to its extreme: If annexation meant war with Mexico, he would rather have "the American soil drenched in the blood of our own people" than "to see the national honor tarnished by tamely submitting to the dictation of any foreign power."[56]

Opposition was found in the debates to the argument that the "Union and its blessings" could "safely" and "beneficially" "spread over the entire continent of North America." But this was expressed in the terms of race and the Texans' unworthiness, along the lines of a *Chicago Tribune* editorial quoted above. Senators argued that the Texans, while not "sordid and treacherous people" like the Mexicans, still represented a threat to the Union, whose real bonds were "those of a common ancestry and a kindred blood."[57] While this "isolationist" trend, constructed as protection of America's uniqueness from foreign contamination, did not prevail in the discussion of foreign affairs on the American continent, it was used to justify nonintervention in the European democratic uprisings.[58] In words echoing the *New York Times* editorials quoted above:

We are not bound to become the Don Quixotes of the age and sally forth to re-dress all the grievances of the civilized world. That has never, so far, been the policy of our country. Greece and Poland had more or less our sympathy, and that was all. We assumed not to decide on the British doings in Afghanistan, or to judge the conduct of the opium war against China. But Texas is our next neighbor, and was once under our special guardianship. We are . . . her nearest friend. To us, if to any nation upon earth, she has a right to look for succor and protection. Shall we forsake her now?[59]

Nevertheless, the United States did have a strong connection with Europe, especially with Great Britain,[60] and in that connection, too, the sense of mission held strong. A victorious continental United States could inspire Europe in its struggle against despotism.[61] It is notewor-thy that the *New York Times* editor wrote in 1859 of the crumbling pa-pal power in Central Italy in these terms: "The 'manifest destiny' appears at length to be about to overtake Rome."[62]

But the United States needed more than expansion to spread the light to the world—it needed expanded communications. One such ef-fort was undertaken in 1858, when the Western Union telegraph com-pany suggested the construction of an overland telegraph line linking Asia and Europe with the United States through the Bering Strait. Sec-retary of State William H. Seward supported the project, saying it would center the United States as the driving force in the extension of civilizing ideals. But the project was abandoned in 1867 because a much more publicized telegraphic enterprise had succeeded—the At-lantic cable had been permanently laid in the meantime.[63]

Cyrus Field, a New York businessman, had promoted the construc-tion of a cable linking North America with Great Britain since 1854, when he established the New York, Newfoundland & London Electric Telegraph Company, with the exclusive right to build ocean cables.[64] Field then sought support in England, where in 1856 the Atlantic Tele-graph Company was formed; Field also convinced the British govern-ment to provide financial aid to the project, with the clause that its messages would have priority over all others, except those of the United States if its government entered upon a similar agreement.[65] Early in 1857, Field went to Washington to ask the U.S. government to do just that, but a bill providing aid to the enterprise met with great difficulties and escaped defeat by one vote in the Senate before being signed into law by President Pierce in March.[66] (After numerous attempts, the ca-ble between Newfoundland and Ireland was laid in August 1858, and though it worked only until September, it was greeted by national celebrations.)

The following pages examine the constructions of foreign countries in the congressional discussions about the bill to aid the construction of "an electric girdle around the world" in January 1857. It should be noted that the cable was introduced as a governmental tool, and support was encouraged on the grounds of "the great international interests of this Government, and the constant occurrence of grave questions, in the solution of which time will be an essential element."[67]

The discussion revolved around the construction of Great Britain as a potential enemy to whom no advantages should be given. Both opponents and supporters of the bill discussed it in terms of the competition with England and its empire, and argued that the cable would either put England at a decisive advantage in war, or it would foster equality and peace. The exclusion of other countries from this discussion is in itself illuminating as to the image the congressmen had of the rest of the world: Even when they discussed the measure from the perspective of commerce, the contest remained exclusively between Great Britain with its colonies and the United States with its territories.[68] As Senator Thomas J. Rusk, of Texas, one of the bill's sponsors, said: "We are dependent upon the foreign market, and we have an immeasurably greater interest in the foreign market than Great Britain or her subjects have in the markets of the United States."[69]

Proponents of the bill said the contract with the English government was formulated so as to indicate that "they seem to desire that the Government of the United States should be put on precisely the same footing with themselves" and that the invitation to join in the effort was tendered "in the spirit of amity." They added that the likelihood of war between the two countries would decrease immensely once the cable was laid because its "cords of iron" would hold the countries "in the bonds of peace." Senator Rusk's words epitomize this view:

If we have no intercourse with foreign nations; if it is not a matter of importance for us to know anything of the political affairs of foreign countries, then we have no interest as a Government in it. If it is not important for us, we have been pursuing a foolish course, for we are spending a great sum of money in sustaining a large diplomatic corps at different places to obtain political information for the use of our Government. . . . The advantages of this work will be mutual, and they must be mutual, between the United States and Great Britain. It is impossible for one nation at this age to get a great advantage over another in means of communication, because, when a communication is made, it will be open to the intelligence and the capital of all.[70]

Opponents of the bill argued the cable gave England power in time of war "to attack and lay waste the whole of the northern States of this Republic."[71] They said the cable was useless because it could not be trusted in time of war, and therefore it could never be used in "foreign intercourse," a position suggesting that war defined, in their view, the extent of U.S. foreign policy. Senator George Pugh, of Ohio, was the most vocal opponent of the bill on the grounds that the cable would extend British global power to an extreme highly detrimental to the United States:

While [England] lectures us privately, and through her newspapers, on the wickedness of our aggressive tendencies, on our disposition to seize the weak States of Central America and Mexico—she is busily engaged in helping herself to slice after slice in the East Indies and Asia. . . . When I see a policy which aspires to control all the affairs of Europe—a policy which by union with France dictates terms in the case of all the intestine quarrels of the European Powers . . . when it is added to a course of aggression and control in Asia, and is to be pursued by strengthening her power and domain upon this continent, on both sides of us . . . I am not disposed, for one, at any instigation, to give her the power of extending any further.[72]

While the discussion seems then to have revolved on notions of international ranking and the need of the United States to defend itself from a hostile power, supporters of the bill also spoke of the cable in terms of mission: "It will be useful and valuable in peace, subservient to the great cause of the advancement of civilization and the diffusion of information"; and "American genius . . . has discovered the principle, and devised the means . . . of sending the principles of American freedom, in the language of Shakespeare, around the globe."[73] On the contrary, opponents of the bill took the continentalist stance and argued that it was much more important to secure communication "between our Atlantic and Pacific coasts, than to communicate with the British coast."[74] Ultimately, the dominant construction of foreign countries in the congressional discussion about aid for the Atlantic cable seems to have been that of war-prone powers (England almost exclusively), which should not be put in a position to prevail over the United States. The only significant difference with editorial constructions seems to be that policymakers emphasized to an even greater degree the threat represented by the foreign powers and the need for the United States to prove its worth.

In conclusion, assuming that congressional debates and editorials can be taken as indicators of cultural understandings, the context of the understanding of foreign realities in the United States between 1838–1859 focused on American superiority and some interpretation of a sense of mission. It seemingly assumed that destiny had put the United States in its leading position, and constructed the world (somewhat ambivalently) as both in need to reckon with that fact and to realize its best hopes by trying to rise to the American standard. The only true dichotomy was between American and non-American; the only difference in the constructions of Europe and the Americas was that proximity made intervention, rather than example, the preferred mission. The following chapters discuss how the first American correspondents abroad constructed this "world" outside the United States. Chapter 5 is devoted to discourses in the eight mainstream newspapers selected and their evolution over time, while Chapter 6 discusses alternative discourses as found in the writings of women correspondents and a black newspaper, as well as relevant background on women in journalism and the black press.

NOTES

1. *New York Times*, September 1, 1859, p. 4.
2. *New York Herald*, May 5, 1859, p. 4.
3. *New York Herald*, July 3, 1845, p. 2, and May 8, 1845, p. 2.
4. *New Orleans Picayune*, January 2, 1845, p. 1.
5. *New Orleans Picayune*, November 4, 1852, p. 2.
6. *New York Herald*, May 8, 1845, p. 2.
7. *New York Herald*, January 6, 1859, p. 4.
8. *New York Herald*, May 9, 1845, p. 2.
9. *New York Herald*, January 7, 1859, p. 4; March 3, 1859, p. 4.
10. *New York Herald*, May 6, 1859, p. 4; July 8, 1859, p. 4.
11. *New York Times*, July 23, 1852, p. 2.
12. *New York Times*, July 23, 1852, p. 2.
13. *New York Herald*, July 23, 1838, p. 2.
14. *New York Herald*, March 6, 1845, p. 2.
15. *New York Herald*, May 6, 1852, p. 4. The *New York Times* editor also spoke indulgently of an Irish rebellion, referring to Belfast as "the home and hot-bed of intolerance"; January 6, 1859, p. 4; the same paper referred to free blacks in the Caribbean islands as "almost entirely animal"; November 3, 1859, p. 4.
16. *Chicago Tribune*, July 7, 1859, p. 2 and January 6, 1853, p. 2.
17. *New Orleans Picayune*, November 7, 1845, p. 1.
18. *New York Herald*, July 2, 1852, p. 4. Another *New York Herald* editorial on Mexico was entitled, "What is to become of that impoverished and misgoverned people?"; *New York Herald*, September 3, 1852, p. 4.

19. *New Orleans Picayune*, May 6, 1859, p. 1.

20. *New York Times*, December 1, 1852, p. 4.

21. *New York Times*, January 7, 1859, p. 4; May 5, 1859, p. 4. The *New York Herald* in 1838 had similarly argued that Canada's problems could not be ignored because of its proximity:

It is but natural the people of the United States should desire to see every country possess political institutions as free as their own. . . . The long and bloody wars that formerly agitated Europe . . . have taught the people of the present day a valuable lesson. They are less bloody-minded—have no desire to see their fellow creatures butchered, either in hot or cold blood. [But] it is not as if these men [the Patriots] had created a rebellion in the heart of England, or in one of her colonies far removed from us. (December 6, 1838, p. 2)

22. *Boston Transcript*, September 2, 1859, p. 2. Also *New York Times*, March 4, 1859, p. 4, Italians felt the government of Rome as "a disgrace to their manhood."

23. *Boston Transcript*, January 6, 1859, p. 2.

24. *New York Tribune*, July 7, 1859, p. 4.

25. *New York Times*, September 2, 1859, p. 4.

26. *Chicago Tribune*, May 6, 1859, p. 2.

27. Editors might also not have perceived the war in Europe as a direct threat to U.S. business interests; this seems to be the case in the *New York Times* editorial that reads: "Up to the present moment the war in Italy has been waged without really embarrassing in any grave degree the serious commercial concerns of the world," *New York Times*, July 8, 1859, p. 4.

28. *New York Times*, July 7, 1859, p. 4.

29. *Boston Transcript*, July 7, 1859, p. 2; *Chicago Tribune*, July 8, 1859, p. 2.

30. *New York Tribune*, May 6, 1859, p. 4.

31. *New York Herald*, March 4, 1859, p. 4; September 2, 1859, p. 4.

32. *Boston Transcript*, July 8, 1859, p. 2.

33. *New Orleans Picayune*, March 4, 1859, p. 1.

34. *New York Herald*, May 6, 1859, p. 4.

35. As early as July 1852, a *New York Tribune* correspondent from Berlin had foreshadowed such conflict: "The question is whether the German or the Russian world, after the downfall of the old civilization (for nothing is more certain than this downfall), will decide the character of the new civilization"; *New York Tribune*, July 2, 1852, p. 6.

36. *New York Herald*, September 2, 1852, p. 4; *New York Tribune*, March 4, 1852, p. 4 and September 2, 1859, p. 4.

37. The use of discourse in diplomatic history has been encouraged by Frank Ninkovich, "Interests and Discourse in Diplomatic History," *Diplomatic History*, 13:2 (spring 1989): 135–161.

38. W. Phillips Davison, Donald R. Shanor, and Frederick T.C. Yu, *News from Abroad and the Foreign Policy Public* (New York: Foreign Policy Association, 1980).

39. Bernard Cohen, *The Press and Foreign Policy* (Princeton, N.J.: Princeton University Press, 1963); James Reston, *The Artillery of the Press* (New York: Harper & Row, 1967); Martin Linsky, *Impact: How the Press Affects Federal Policymaking* (New York: W.W. Norton, 1986); William A. Dorman and Mansour Farhang, *The U.S. Press and Iran: Foreign Policy and the Journalism of Deference* (Berkeley: University of California Press, 1987).

40. Nicholas Berry, *Foreign Policy and the Press* (Westport, Conn.: Greenwood Press, 1990). Also, Michael Fibison compared U.S. news about a foreign country with U.S. State Department policies toward it and he found that the elite media promoted the "establishment's" foreign policy in their reporting about the country. In Michael D. Fibison, *The Cold War Facade*, M.A. thesis, University of Minnesota, 1997.

41. Roger S. Whitcomb, *The American Approach to Foreign Affairs* (Westport, Conn.: Praeger, 1998): 52–53, 128–131 especially.

42. Michael H. Hunt, *Ideology and U.S. Foreign Policy* (New Haven, Conn.: Yale University Press, 1987): 13, 21.

43. Charles Vevier, "American Continentalism: An Idea of Expansion, 1845–1910," *American Historical Review* 65:2 (1960): 323–335.

44. Rush Welter, *The Mind of America, 1820–1860* (New York: Columbia University Press, 1975): 66.

45. Welter, p. 73.

46. The information for this brief summary of American foreign policy is derived from Alexander Deconde, *A History of American Foreign Policy*. 3rd ed. Vol.1(New York: Charles Scribner's Sons, 1978): 134–221.

47. Hunt, p. 35.

48. Varg argues that some of the key foreign policymakers were "errand boys of business"; Paul Varg, *United States Foreign Relations, 1820–1860* (East Lansing: Michigan State University Press, 1979): 206, also 76, 195, 287. Also, William A. Williams, *The Roots of the Modern American Empire* (New York: Random House, 1969).

49. Ernest May, *American Imperialism* (New York: Atheneum, 1968); Kinley Brauer, "The United States and British Imperial Expansion, 1815–60," *Diplomatic History*, 12:1 (1988): 19–37.

50. Frederick Merk, *Manifest Destiny and Mission in American History* (New York: Alfred A. Knopf, 1963): 24, 31, 121.

51. Merk, pp. 4, 34–35, 56–57.

52. Norman Graebner, *Foundations of American Foreign Policy* (Wilmington, Del.: Scholarly Resources, 1985): 190, 192.

53. *Congressional Globe*, 28 Cong., 2nd sess., pp. 84–363 (January 3 to February 27, 1845).

54. David Pletcher, *The Diplomacy of Annexation* (Columbia: University of Missouri Press, 1973): 5.

55. *Congressional Globe*, 28 Cong., 2nd sess., pp. 86, 336, 343.

56. *Congressional Globe*, 28 Cong., 2nd sess., pp. 87, 119. More pragmatically, Senator Allen argued that the United States needed Texas to be able to compete in the "direct rivalry for commercial ascendancy" with Great Britain, p. 342.

57. *Congressional Globe*, 28 Cong., 2nd sess., pp. 111, 183, 282.

58. Welter, p. 69.

59. *Congressional Globe*, 28 Cong., 2nd sess., p. 112.

60. See Frank Thistlethwaite, *The Anglo-American Connection in the Early Nineteenth Century* (Philadelphia: University of Pennsylvania Press, 1959).

61. Merk, p. 201.

62. *New York Times*, March 4, 1859, p. 4.

63. Charles Vevier, "The Collins Overland Line and American Continentalism," *Pacific Historical Review* 28:3 (1959): 237–253.

64. Robert L. Thompson, *Wiring a Continent* (Princeton, N.J.: Princeton University Press, 1947): 299–300.

65. Henry Field, *History of the Atlantic Telegraph* (New York: Charles Scribner & Co., 1867): 93–97.

66. Field, pp. 108–130.

67. See *Congressional Globe*, 34 Cong., 3rd sess. (January 10 to 22, 1857): 257–425; 394.

68. *Congressional Globe*, 34 Cong., 3rd sess., especially p. 418.

69. *Congressional Globe*, 34 Cong., 3rd sess., p. 399.

70. *Congressional Globe*, 34 Cong., 3rd sess., pp. 395, 396, 398.

71. *Congressional Globe*, 34 Cong., 3rd sess., p. 396.

72. *Congressional Globe*, 34 Cong., 3rd sess., p. 416.

73. *Congressional Globe*, 34 Cong., 3rd sess., p. 424.

74. *Congressional Globe*, 34 Cong., 3rd sess., p. 397.

CHAPTER 5

CONSTRUCTIONS OF THE "WORLD" IN THE MAINSTREAM PRESS

The earliest American correspondents created meanings about the foreign realities they wrote about within the discursive boundaries of American superiority and mission. Some of the constructions—especially that of the beautiful, bountiful country misgoverned by its unskilled inhabitants—reflect those found in the editorials and foreign policy discussions identified in the previous chapter. The most intriguing finding of this study, however, is that the constructions in foreign correspondence tend to be significantly more ambivalent, even contradictory, in the meanings they create about foreign countries. That clear empathy for the uniqueness of a local culture and even harsh criticism of American policies and prejudices could exist within articles imbued with the themes of condescension and belief in American superiority suggests that the correspondents did make a difference in how a commonsense understanding of the "world" developed in nineteenth-century America.

Even though correspondence was not free from stereotypes (particularly racial), the correspondents, perhaps because of greater familiarity with their subject matter, showed a better understanding of native cultures than did U.S. congressmen and editors at home. Several writers were apparently conversant in the main European languages; Taylor seems to have been able to read Arabic.[1] As the form of foreign correspondence evolved from the earlier travel letter type to the later, detailed political and social analyses, correspondents seem to have struggled with ingrained frames of reference for foreign cultures and their own, often contradictory experiences abroad. Hardly a construction was found without a contradiction in another or even the same story. The following excerpt from Bayard Taylor's comment upon his feelings at witnessing an Islamic celebration in Istanbul illustrates: "It was a picture of air—a phantasmagoria built of luminous vapor and meteoric fires, and hanging in the dark round of space. *In spite of ourselves* we became eager and excited"[2] [italics added]. Conflict between a definite empathy with the foreign cultures and the larger sense of American mission seems apparent in statements by several correspondents that qualify the occasional admiration as "in spite of themselves."

While at least one letter from a foreign correspondent was found in each newspaper studied, the amounts varied greatly, with the New York newspapers clearly dominating; hence, most examples here come from the New York papers. In the four years (at intervals) studied, only one travel letter was found in the *Chicago Tribune* (in 1853); two each were found in the *Boston Transcript* and the *Missouri Republican* (in 1852 and 1859); and three in the *Charleston Courier* (in 1838, 1852, and 1859). The *New Orleans Picayune* had the most stories among the non-New York papers, with five letters found for 1859 alone. These numbers are significant when compared to the three New York dailies—in 1859 alone, this research found the *Tribune* had twelve letters from foreign correspondents, the *Times* had seventeen and the *Herald* was the leader with thirty-seven.

Almost all of the correspondence read was written in either western Europe or Latin America (especially Mexico and the Central American countries), though a few letters came from the Middle and Far East and northern Africa. The earlier correspondence, often written in the style of literary journalism (descriptive, witty, and critical), provides an even better ground for examining discursive constructions than would strictly factual reporting.[3] The 1859 correspondence, especially that from Europe, tends more toward the analytical than the descriptive, perhaps because of the complexities of the war and the power arrangements throughout the continent; nevertheless, it remained significantly different from the "straight" news style exemplified by the digests. Most correspondents throughout the period studied wrote in first person. While the articles vary depending upon the correspondents' individual styles and the country where they were generated, several common constructions are identifiable across the years and the newspapers. Long extracts from the correspondence are provided to best exemplify them.

One of the earliest and most persistent constructions of foreign countries compared any observed object (ranging from the British press to the dust on British trains and even rain showers)[4] with an American counterpart. Comparison is to be expected in the creation of a commonsense understanding about foreign realities, because it explicitly incorporates elements that belong to the public's common knowledge. A *New York Times* correspondent from Piedmont, Italy, wrote that the landscape reminded him "of our Western grain fields," while a *Charleston Courier* correspondent wrote that young boys along the roads in the Swiss Alps played music for travelers on tubes "resembling the horns used by the negro boatmen on our rivers in Carolina."[5] However, most often the comparison was in terms of competition and, with few exceptions, explicitly favored the American version, thus reinforcing a construction of the "world" as inferior to the United States. Bennett's own letters from Europe in 1838 exemplify: "London is not like New York. This is a huge, overgrown place; it is composed of different and distinct communities. New York, on the contrary, has one soul, one mind, one heart, one purpose, one character. Though only one-fifth the size of London, New York has a heart big enough for the world." The ending to another of his letters perfectly sums up the extreme of such an attitude: "In fact, I love and adore New York the more I see of London."[6]

A few comparisons put local cultures at the same level as the culture of the United States; some unequivocally praised the local population. Describing the "well-behaved" and "intelligent young men" of Siena, Italy, who read aloud in the town square the few newspapers they could find, a *New York Herald* correspondent wrote: "it is a scene probably somewhat like what may be witnessed in some of our new settlements"; he also wrote that the members of the assembly of Florence "looked as near like one of our State legislatures proceeding to the opening of a session as any American could desire." The same issue of the *Herald* has a piece from the Paris correspondent who, writing about the Parisians at the celebration of the army of Italy, said: "[They] presented a *coup d'oeil* of well-clothed, well behaved people, such as any nation, whatever its claims to greatness, might be excused for envying."[7] Most comparisons favoring other cultures reveal a sense of admiration for the supposed cultural superiority of the Old World, as the following shows: "This salon [at Palazzo Vecchio in Florence], by the grandeur of its proportions and majestic general aspect, puts to shame all monuments of our Anglo-Saxon pride of a similar character."[8] But in some cases, as in the *New York Tribune* correspondence from Greece and Italy that follows, even an artistic comparison seems to fall within the discourse of American superiority:

The coast certainly offers nothing to justify the high notions one has formed of the Epirus, Arcadia, and the Peloponnesus of Ancient Greece. One would never dream that this was the home of gods, heroes and poets. Arcadian groves are parched, deserted, destroyed. The people are ignorant, lazy, miserable, half-naked, and would be mistaken in our country for a tribe of Pawnee Indians. . . . Ah, give me the life and freshness of "my own, my dear native hills!" Give me the practical utilitarianism of our living age—an age which looks to the real improvement of the race! . . . If Homer could make such rough and rugged desolation sing the songs of delight . . . there certainly must be Helicons as pure in the fresh vitality of our own favored land. . . . I love to hear these people grumble against the oppressions of despotic governments. I love to hear them inquire about our own. It proves that the leaven is working. The whole lump will rise by and bye. . . . These old masters [in Florence museums], great and necessary as they were in their day, have not half reached the point art will sometime arrive at, and are in general much overrated. . . . It remains to be wished that our artists, after having carefully examined the works of these masters—instead of continuing here for ever [*sic*] copying them—would return to the yet unpainted grandeur of our own mountains, prairies and races for their models, and assuredly more originality, force, and fame, will be theirs.[9]

Not surprisingly, one of Bennett's own letters eulogized American theater: "It has been supposed that any worn-out London actor would do well enough for the United States. . . . The time is rapidly coming when we will give actors to the London stage. Genius and talent in that line can find a better opening on our side than on this. We have no prejudices—no set opinions, to interpose obstacles in the path of young adventurers."[10] Similarly, the only correspondence found in the *Chicago Tribune* dealt with a contrast between European art and the prospects for similar achievements in the United States:

In real, useful and utilitarian efforts, and at small burthen of cost, we are comparatively far ahead of the Old World in many ways, and in the blending of taste with economy we also in many things excel them. But in the splendor of their structures, and in the fine arts, we shall never equal them with our present institutions and notions. It is despotism and absolute power in church and state, or overgrown wealth in the hands of the few; broad distinctions in classes, want of occupation with the wealthy and aristocratic, the necessity for excitement, and the desire for ostentatious display to mark more widely the difference between the privileged and their inferiors, which lead to such large expenditures in palaces, cathedrals, and churches, pictures, and statuary, and in ornamental grounds etc. etc. I do not see how we shall ever concentrate funds for a Louvre or a Versailles.[11]

"Buncle," *New York Times* correspondent from France and Germany in 1852, poked fun at writing in comparative terms, despite doing it himself quite often; in fact, his comparisons, ostensibly favorable to America, might indeed be contradictory and subtly critical of Americans:

To a German, a vineyard, with its associations, lyric and gustative, is one of the most agreeable objects that eye can rest upon. To the naked visual organs of an unsophisticated American, it has no attractions: it lacks the waving grace of our rich corn-fields—is hardly distinguishable from a field of pole-beans. . . . The hurrah raised by the crowd assembled to greet [the king's] arrival at Coblentz was quite the best "specimen" in its kind that I have heard in Europe; it even approached an American hurrah, undoubtedly the finest variety in the world of this species of demonstration. . . . Freedom of intercourse, one may here say literally, between Prince and peasant, is less restricted than between the old-family Browns and the new-family Joneses, of our Republican watering places. . . . I envy them their German faculty of leisurely enjoyment of taking in pleasure so calmly—as it were, slowly chewing the cud of it for days together, instead of bolting it quickly, in our Am—But, enough of comparisons.[12]

A condescending tone of superiority, particularly political, permeated some comparisons, and recurred throughout most correspondence read. Bennett, for example, wrote in 1838 of his conversation with an Englishman:

"Yours is a beautiful country," said I—"It's highly cultivated—every valley is a garden—every little hill a paradise, but it is all in miniature. It seems as if I could put my hand from this coach, and, stretching it over these lovely fields, hide them from the light of day. It seems that a pocket kerchief hung up before the rising sun, would bury all Devonshire in darkness. [England] is a lovely, rich, cultivated country, but a Kentuckian could put it into his breeches pocket, and almost button the flap upon it."[13]

The same *New York Herald* correspondent who in 1859 had put the Tuscan Assembly on the same level as an American legislature went on to say the Assembly proved that "the population emerged from a condition of political childhood or servitude to the dignity and responsibility of manhood."[14] In a few instances, such condescension turned into ridicule of foreign cultures, as when a *New York Tribune* correspondent called the treaty of Vienna "the most monstrous *fictiones iuris publici* ever heard of in the annals of mankind" and when his colleague in Paris wrote "it is a comfort to fish out, at last, this one fact from the sea of words that has been swelling, waste and watery, about the green table of the Hotel Baur at Zurich."[15] The same Paris correspondent illustrates in another instance this tongue-in-cheek attitude toward foreign policies, in this case Louis Napoleon's general amnesty:

How it comes that a man who was a justly punished wretch the day before the 15th of August, or the birth-day of an Imperial prince, or the coronation day of a prince succeeding his dead father, and would have so remained if the fête had not been appointed or the boy had been a girl, or the old king had got well—how it comes about, I say, that such wonderful purgatorial or reforming virtue should belong to these apparently chronological and physical accidents, is to your correspondent an unsolved ethical problem.[16]

Condescension also took the form of stereotypes, with which some correspondents stamped either European leaders ("Lord Chandos is a plain, plodding and somewhat pettifogging specimen of the modern ducal breed") or peoples of different races (referring to the Zouave battalions of the French army as "tigers," "simple-minded Algerians" who "love the taste of blood").[17] The anti-Austrian bias, observed in editorials in Chapter 4, was also particularly strong among correspondents in 1859; the London correspondent of the *New York Herald* reported that Austria was acting with "characteristic stupidity."[18] Correspondents for the *New York Tribune* did not spare harsh words for the Austrians, both in the frontlines and in the political leadership. A writer from Turin stated: "Impossibilities did not exist for the Austrian officers. . . . If only half of what I have been told is true, the sojourn of many of these officers must have been an uninterrupted series of knavish tricks and acts of wantonness, committed on purpose to try to the utmost the patience of their inoffensive hosts"; a colleague in London wrote that "Austria in the mean while [*sic*], is sinking day by day into a lower depth of disrepute."[19]

The widespread image of foreign leaders as incapable, or worse, was found in two interrelated constructions—American uniqueness and superiority (particularly political), noted above, and the inability of foreign countries to exploit their resources on their own. Obviously, this second construction relates to the sense of mission and the Manifest Destiny doctrine discussed in regard to the editorials, for these notions were based on assumptions that other countries have the potential for rising to the American level both politically and economically, but not if left to themselves. Such discourse about foreign cultures as bountiful but enslaved and incapable of self-government, and therefore necessitating American intervention, was expressed explicitly. These excerpts illustrate: "The Nile offers a perpetual fountain of plenty and prosperity, and its long valley, from Nubia to the sea, would become, *in other hands*, the garden of the world"; "The Turks are a people easy to govern. They would thrive and improve under a better state of things, but I can't help feeling the conviction that the regeneration of the East will never be effected *at their hands* [italics added]."[20] But the same discourse was also implicit in the dichotomous construction of beauty/strife: "The present unsettled state of that fine island [St. Domingo] is deplorable; fertile and blooming in agricultural riches, the luxuriant fruits of the soil are wasted by the folly of men."[21]

Often, the construction was both paternalistic and sympathetic, especially when the correspondents excoriated foreign leaders because they supposedly mistreated their own peoples. For example, a *New York Times* correspondent wrote in 1852: "Behold, my dear friends, by what wretched and criminal crowned heads is ruled beautiful Italy. . . . Tuscany, the native country of Dante, has fallen under the most revolting despotism."[22] Another *New York Times* correspondent, writing from Istanbul about the vast industry of leech export, echoed this construction: "The young [leeches] sustain life by sucking the blood of their mother and this trait in the natural history of the animal may lead you . . . to find new analogies between the relations of governors and subjects in Turkey, and the unvarying instinct of the leech, that is never satisfied, but from the very beginning is crying, 'Give, give.' "[23] Another *Times* correspondent, from Mexico City, wrote scathingly in 1859 of the clergy ruling in Mexico, saying that the "poor Indians" looked upon a locomotive "with more wonder" than upon the Virgin of Guadalupe, and "if the holy fathers had the power to give it a supernatural character, the poor ignorant creatures would fall down and worship it."[24] "Azul," writing from Havana for the *Charleston Courier*, argued: "The political position of Venezuela is positively distressing. The entire country appears to be overrun with revolutionary bandits, who sack, burn and destroy the property and take the lives of the peaceable inhabitants."[25] A *New York Herald* correspondent in 1859 thus chastised both Louis Napoleon and the "gullible" French people:

The Emperor, notwithstanding his public disclaimer from the throne not so long ago, of the reputed necessity of an occasional *coup de theatre* for the due government of the French people, always takes excellent care, in the absence of any important event, that some subject more or less piquant shall be thrown down, as a sop to Cerberus, on which the French mind may amuse itself till something more substantial can be provided. Right now it is Count Cavour's despatch on the massacre perpetuated by the Austrian Field Marshal Urban, which keeps the war thermometer from sinking too low.[26]

In other instances, the theme that a country cannot be expected to better itself on its own involved the construction not just of inept or corrupt leadership but of the whole people as totally incapable of self-government—a clear proto-imperialistic notion. In addition to the example of the native population infesting Algeria cited in Chapter 1,[27] Bayard Taylor, usually rather sympathetic to foreign cultures, wrote of Arabs as disturbing their own towns by their very presence: "The silence and aspect of desertion harmonize well with the spirit of the [temple], which would be much disturbed, were one beset, as is usual in the Arab towns, by a gang of naked beggars and barking wolf-dogs."[28] Not too dissimilarly, Henry Howard wrote from Germany in 1852 of the dejected state of affairs in the country, adding a venomous word about the treatment of Americans abroad:

With all the good qualities which the Germans individually possess, they lack every one necessary to a nation—true patriotism, self-esteem, devotion to their country, is foreign to them; instead of which they are full of degrading submissiveness to every one who bears the title of a prince, or belongs to the aristocracy; the next to the throne is more a slave than our negroes in the South. . . . The Germans will grumble and complain vehemently of the despotism which presses them down, but, like a well-whipped dog, they will lay down at the feet of their princely master. . . . Those who differ from them, and consider the princes as their equal born, have already or are about emigrating to our happy country. . . . All that vexes the princely rulers and their satellites, is the freedom the British, but, in particular, we, the Americans, enjoy, and that they have no power to deprive us thereof. Viper like, they let their spite out against innocent travellers.[29]

Such a construction has as a corollary that the country in question needs foreign intervention to be saved from itself; a correspondent from Kingston, Jamaica, wrote in 1859 that "the general desire is that additional soldiers shall be sent to the island" lest "the lower orders" "elect some ignorant negro as their governor in chief."[30] An 1859 report from another correspondent, from Argentina, exemplifies the benevolent mission construction. It sums up in a sentence the discourse of foreign inferiority and the condescending, helpful American attitude: "South America is in its infancy, and infancy requires occasional indulgences and occasional chastisings."[31] It is important to note that the opposite construction existed—the *New York Herald* Italian correspondent wrote that the best results would come if European powers left Tuscany and Central Italy alone: "If there is no armed interference by France or Austria in Central Italy, the people will elect their rulers, establish a government, and peacefully adjust all their affairs, not only after the wishes of their own hearts but in a manner to satisfy the reasonable public opinion of Europe."[32] Taylor, accompanying the U.S. mission to open trade with Japan, wrote in 1858 from that country for the *New York Tribune*: "To the Japanese themselves, I do not for a moment suppose that intercourse with foreigners will be a blessing. . . . Rigidly honest in their dealings, they will take neither more nor less than what they consider the value of an article. Intercourse with foreigners will no doubt rectify this evil."[33]

Of the correspondence studied, only that in the *New York Herald* showed constructions of foreign countries (especially on the American continent) explicitly reflecting the dominant discourse found in editorials and foreign policy discussion—annexation or intervention are necessary to those countries' own benefit. The Caracas, Venezuela, correspondent asked in 1859: "Will foreign governments remain passive and submit to such imposition and gross robberies from a people who are entirely incapable of managing their own affairs?" The Mexico City correspondent wrote that assassinations and mistreatment of foreigners would continue because "so the game goes, and so it will go until we get some positive support from abroad." Possibly the same correspondent, writing from Veracruz just a few months later, impatiently summed up the pro-annexation stand: "Nothing short of an American army can put an end to the [Mexican civil] struggle, do what you please. If this cannot be obtained, everything will go to the dogs and no mistake."[34] The following 1852 article from Montreal illustrates that this Manifest Destiny discourse was not applied only to South America and to non-Anglo ethnicities:

The present generation of the mass of Canadians are as ignorant of the benefits of a free government, as were their French ancestors two hundred years ago. There is no improvement in their condition, either mentally, morally, or politically; and they are as subservient to the priesthood and monarchy under which they live, as are the subjects of the most despotic government on earth. They pursue the same plodding course of their early ancestors, living a dull, heavy,

laborious, monotonous life. . . . In the cities of Toronto, Kingston, and Montreal, however, the light of intelligence is now making rapid progress. I had frequent, full, open, and free conversations with many of their leading men . . .
these leading men are strong and emphatic in their desire for annexation to the
United States. . . . Annexation is desired by them, in order that the immense resources of Canada may become developed. They desire it also, that their people, who have ever been the slaves to tyranny in many features, may experience
the great blessings of independence and freedom. . . . The Canadians entertain
no idea of remaining a sovereign power; they are aware of themselves, they are
lamentably deficient in the elements of self-government.[35]

An explicitly anti-annexation discourse was found in an 1859 *New
York Tribune* article from London; though critical of British colonization, the correspondent did attack the myth of colonization as enlightenment: "According to his oracle in Printing-House Square, [the
British] grasps after colonies only in order to educate them in the principles of public liberty; but, if we adhere to facts, the Ionian Islands, like
India and Ireland, prove only that to be free at home, John Bull must
enslave abroad."[36] "C.D.," however, *Herald* correspondent from
Belize, writing in 1852 about Great Britain's occupation of islands off
that coast, also criticized British colonialism—but only to introduce the
element of competition in the Manifest Destiny discourse:

Among the intelligent, the question is often asked, "What are the Yankees doing, that they should allow this step on the part of Great Britain?" . . . It requires no great stretch of imagination to see this continent, in a very few years,
a part of your Union. Its situation, and everything else, has been fitted by nature for it, and not many years can elapse before this entire continent will be a
part and parcel of the United States. The people desire it.[37]

A related construction, found predominantly in foreign policy debates, appeared in some foreign correspondence. Though much less
prominent, this was the construction of the unstable, politically inferior
status of foreign countries as directly threatening the United States,
whose power other countries need to be reminded of. All of this, of
course, again suggests the necessity and morality of U.S. intervention.
A *New York Herald* Havana correspondent wrote in 1859 that "another instance of the ridiculousness of Spanish law" "seriously inconve-
nienced" an American.[38] The theme of outside threat to the United
States can be seen in the earliest correspondence found in the *New Orleans Picayune*. In 1845, the correspondent wrote:

Dear Pic—Presuming that you are always gratified to hear from your Yankee friends residing in this little village, called London, I venture to scribble a few lines for the purpose of warning you against a war fever that has suddenly broken out in England, and asking you and your good citizens to prepare your cotton bales for a bombardment! I am in earnest. . . . [John Bull] now frets and foams, and declares that nothing short of a sound trashing can keep "the bullying Americans" quiet! . . . My only advice to Mr. President Polk and his Cabinet is—don't allow John Bull to catch you all asleep![39]

When not portrayed as threatening, other countries were portrayed as ignorant of the United States and its power. Correspondence in 1852 from Montreal, noted above for its pro-annexation stance, illustrates: "It is a matter of much regret, that the social intercourse between the people of the United States and the Canadians has so long been neglected and comparatively restricted. We are astonished at the ignorance which prevails, even amongst the best informed, of the principles of the U.S. government, its wealth, resources and power."[40] Much along the same lines, a *New York Times* correspondent from Mexico City in 1859 linked the Mexicans' supposed anti-American sentiments to their inherent unworthiness: "What have we to hope from a people whose ignorance and vulgarity are excused when these things can be construed as aimed against the Yankees?"[41] "R.W.R.," also of the *Times*, wrote in 1859 that in Tyrol there was "universal curiosity and wonderful ignorance" about everything American.[42]

The opposite of this construction also was found in the correspondence. Several writers acknowledged that foreign peoples had a great interest in, and admiration for, the United States—though this could also be seen as belonging to the discourse of supposed American superiority. Bennett, in letters from London in 1838, while remaining characteristically patriotic, contradicted so many of his own later editorials by writing: "One thing is certain—this country has a higher opinion of the United States than we had been taught to believe. . . . In this country, wherever I have been as yet, the real, natural, bold, plump American character always commands the greatest respect and esteem. . . . The more I see of this country the more I am satisfied that the United States is only in the beginning of her career."[43]

"Buncle" of the *Times* wrote in 1852 that, because of the great number of German immigrants to the United States, an American in Germany is welcomed everywhere:

Any American had, indeed, a two-fold advantage over other foreigners traveling in this country. His mere title of American citizen, partly just because he can bear no other, gives him whatever social rank his manners and education qualify him to sustain; and being both democrat and sovereign, he is allowed to take place where he wills. Then, again, wherever he goes, he is welcomed as a bearer of tidings from the Western Land of Promise.[44]

A *Herald* correspondent from St. Petersburg wrote in 1859 that "everything American" was "quite popular" in Russia.[45] Clearly upon second thought, perhaps with an eye to pleasing his editor by showing foreign respect for America, a *Herald* Paris correspondent added at the bottom of an 1859 letter written three days after the one describing the grand entry of the army of Italy: "In my description of the *fêtes* I ought to have mentioned that the stripes and star spangled banner proved a very conspicuous feature upon the houses by which the grand military procession passed."[46]

An 1859 letter from "Gamma," of the *New Orleans Picayune* in Paris, contains most of the constructions discussed thus far—the world is in a troubled state, because of misgoverned, violence-prone peoples, and the United States needs to hold tight to the continent so as to prove its uniqueness and power:

In what a state of confusion is Europe! At Constantinople, a great conspiracy to overthrow the existing order of things; the Italian peninsula, seething with revolution from one end to the other, and at Parma reproducing some of the worst traits of 1849; Spain building up a great army, and schooling it in Africa; France arming and fortifying, and its population excited to increased hatred of England, by song book and newspaper article; a growing feeling in France that the present Government has not long to live [*I speak this advisedly.* I could startle you with some opinions I have heard expressed in strict confidence]; the ferment on the Southern shores of the Mediterranean; all bode signs of a coming tempest—tornado, rather, which will shake Europe to depths the convulsion of 1848 itself did not reach. War! war! war! is coming, the people think, and the Teutonic and Latin races are going to battle for the mastership of the world, as if there was not across the stormy Atlantic, *a great nation which can cope single handed against the world*, and never will permit Canada or the sugar islands to be held by any hands other than kindred Teutons.[47] [second italics added]

But, as noted, foreign correspondence, pervaded as it was by the sense of mission, the doctrine of Manifest Destiny, and American superiority, at times reflected parodies of those constructions. The following passage, by a *New York Times* correspondent in Minatitlan, Mexico, in 1859 illustrates; after writing about the dejected state of the country and the incident of mail stolen out of spite for "los Yankees," the writer sarcastically added: "We are, of course, looking for some naval demonstration here immediately, to avenge this insult to our national dignity."[48] Even more than ridiculing American paranoia about affronts to national pride, many correspondents wrote correspondence that shows a genuine effort to understand a foreign culture on its own terms and merits, often with great analytical depth and sometimes critical of U.S. policies. The constructions in articles where competing images of the "world" are most evident are the most interesting, and they illustrate the most significant differences between the meanings created in the domestic texts and those constructed by the journalists abroad.

By way of introduction, it is important to reiterate that the correspondents seemed to have recognized their role as providers of analysis of foreign cultures. Nonetheless, even when trying to advise their readers as to possible future movements on the international scene (especially in the conflicts of 1859), they emphasized they were basing their observations on facts. A *New York Tribune* Paris correspondent illustrates; writing in 1859 about the different possibilities of postwar governments in Italy, he appended this disclaimer: "Being in the dark on both hypotheses, I do *not guess*, but *report* and pass on"[49] [italics added]. Indeed, one correspondent the same year parodied the tendency to explain foreign cultures by saying that he was "unendowed by nature with those prophetic powers which she has so freely bestowed on many editors, and on most foreign correspondents."[50] "Dean," writing also in 1859 from Paris for the *New York Times*, lamented the partisanship of *London Times* correspondents in the Italian conflict and alleged that "as a general thing, public opinion in the United States has been too much controlled by the English Press," particularly the *Times*. He asked, as if in support of "independent" foreign correspondence, "Is it not time that Americans be enabled to judge of European matters more fully than by getting only one side of the question, and it a most prejudiced one?"[51]

Several articles of correspondence, especially in the 1850s, painstakingly analyzed international questions and provided readers with context and background so they would not be caught by surprise by developments like war (which critics argued happened nearly a century later with World War I because of the correspondents' strict objectivity).[52] The dense political essay on the influence of Germany on Eastern Europe published in the *New York Tribune* in 1852 and perceptively noting Germany's colonizing aims over eastern Europe, would be a perfect example were it not anomalous in regard to its authorship—it was written by Karl Marx, correspondent from London.[53]

But an article in the *New York Herald* the same year on internal European politics is perhaps even more noteworthy. Europe is portrayed as the site of conflict, but in highly informative (even prophetic) terms, not necessarily as serving the mission construction discussed above. "B.H.R." from Paris wrote in 1852: "Whoever looks at the condition of Europe, cannot fail to see that before the lapse of many years, the torch of war will be lighted up anew, and the political and commercial interests of every nation be put at hazard. It is more than probable that all the great international questions, interests, and principles, will again, as heretofore, be decided upon the ocean."[54] Political analysis was not limited to the larger corps of correspondents for the New York dailies. "Fidelitas," the Paris correspondent for the *Missouri Republican*, also wrote a detailed essay on politics in France and their expected impact on the balance of power among European nations, while his colleague in London, "D.D.M.," wrote for the same newspaper: "Nothing but a congress of nations, or a general war can dispel the dark clouds which now lower over all Europe."[55]

Analysis of affairs in foreign countries led some correspondents (particularly those of the *New York Times*) to harshly criticize U.S. foreign policies and policymakers' ignorance about foreign cultures. "N.," a *New York Times* correspondent from Buenos Aires, in an article reprinted in 1859 in the *Charleston Courier* blamed the ignorance of Washington leaders in regard to foreign cultures for creating dangerous connections with disreputable South American leaders:

What a pity it is, that amidst the puerile squabbles of party at Washington, our Government has not time to study, ever so little, the questions which divide parties in these countries, and to give orders to our representatives, who come here as ignorant as themselves, that they should not befoul our national reputation by contact with assassins [local dictators], although—for the disgrace of human nature—they may hold temporary power over a portion of their fellow beings.[56]

The same correspondent reiterated that the misguided policy of the American commissioner in Paraguay was "evidence of American ignorance, presumption and bad faith" and that it brought "the blush of shame to my face."[57] "Pericles," in Turin also for the *Times*, found the American minister there uninterested in Italian affairs and wondered, "how long the United States would continue to send abroad as representatives so many mere political demagogues."[58]

In contrast to the supposedly ignorant, uninterested policymakers at home, the foreign correspondents seemed proud of participating in foreign cultures. The *Times* correspondent "Malakoff" wrote about the new Italian anthem: "The Italians ate, drank, went to bed, got up, marched and fought in unison with its notes; *I did the same (all but the fighting) myself.* It is one of those glorious airs which raises a man's heart to the perpendicular and sets his nerves in a tremor. . . . The world owes Italy her independence, if for nothing else than her glorious music"[59] [italics added]. It is not surprising that increased familiarity with a foreign culture should lead to increased empathy and the subsequently better ability to judge a foreign reality on its own terms. For example, two *New York Herald* correspondents in 1859 empathetically described the antiwar sentiment of the German people and the playfully democratic feeling of a Parisian bourgeois crowd who wished to be aristocratic for a day:

Kings and lords and knights and goodly dames were but sensible flesh and blood, why should not the multitude of holiday folk itself occupy their places, and see how they looked reclining on benches of velvet and fauteuils of crimson and gold? To conceive the thought was to realize it, and in a moment some 20,000 of the goodly bourgeois of the capital were installed in the seats of those who but a few hours before would have turned up their noses had they dared so much as to pass bewixt the wind and their nobility.[60]

Most of the correspondence that reflected a sympathetic understanding of foreign cultures was found in the *New York Tribune* and the *New York Times*. However, in virtually all cases, exploring a foreign reality on its own terms clashes with some of the context discussed, namely the American assumption of other nations' inferiority to America and racial or ethnic stereotypes. Therefore, these letters are particularly significant to this study of discourses of the "world" because they represent a site of discursive struggle in which American mission and superiority are both followed and seriously challenged. By questioning these cultural constructions, the first foreign correspondents helped modify the discourse of the "world" in American media.

The struggle often reflected the seeking of an understanding of a local culture while reinforcing the sense of its inferiority to the United States—one construction often appears only a paragraph or two from the other. For example, "Buncle" identified with the German peasantry at a royal spectacle in 1852 only to reaffirm in the same article that the best German achievements could be seen in the United States:

[The illumination] was, in some sort, emblematical of things here in Europe—we commoners setting out a glare of light in front of us to illuminate His Majesty and tickle his royal ears, while our poor subject senses were half suffocated with the stench of burning lard. . . . How would [Gutenberg] feel, could he visit earth, and see the products of his inventions—Leipzig book catalogues, libraries of British museums, *penny newspapers, and American Republics!* [61] [italics added]

Bayard Taylor also showed sympathy toward foreign peoples, as when he described the 1852 celebration of Ramadan's end in Istanbul: "There was no Turk so poor that he did not in some sort share in the rejoicing. Our 'Fourth' [of July] could scarcely show more flags, let off more big guns, or send forth greater crowds of excursionists than this Moslem holiday."[62] However, his correspondence was also contradictory—showing, on the one hand, a seeking for understanding of local cultures on their own terms while exhibiting, on the other hand, a perspective of superiority. In the Egyptian correspondence discussed above in the context of the construction of natives as damaging their own country, one can read a clearly positive statement about the Arab population. Taylor described the prayer rituals as follows:

The process of rising, kneeling, striking their foreheads on the deck, etc., has almost the appearance of a gymnastic exercise, but their devotion is evidently sincere. In the cathedrals of Christian Europe, I have often seen pantomimes quite as unnecessary, performed with less apparent reverence. The people of Egypt are fully as honest and well-disposed as the greater part of the Italian peasantry.[63]

Taylor's portrayal of the Turks, however, was mixed. In one article, some lines put the population on the same level with Europeans and the writer:

The worshippers present [inside Hagia Sophia] looked at us with curiosity, but without ill-will, and before we left one of the priests came slyly with some fragments of the ancient gilded mosaic, which *he was heathen enough to sell and we to buy.* . . . [The mosque of Suleyman the Magnificent] is a type of Oriental, as the Parthenon is of Grecian, and the Cologne Cathedral of Gothic art. As I saw it the other night, lit by the flames of a conflagration, standing out red and clear against the darkness, I felt inclined *to place it on a level with either of those renowned structures.* [italics added]

But, a few lines below in the same article, the discourse of American superiority is again evident in a description of the intervention of American naval officers to quell a devastating fire: "The proceedings of the Americans, who cut holes in the roofs and played through them upon the fires within, were watched by the Turks with stupid amazement: 'Mushallah!' said a fat Bimbashi, as he stood sweltering in the heat, 'The Franks are wonderful people.' "[64]

In passing, it is worthy of note that a locus for ambivalent constructions was the discussion of foreign countries' technological advancements and press systems. While there is appreciation for advances and condemnation for the authoritarian press system, the writers still implicitly compared these foreign realities to American models, which were constructed as the best. To wit, the following backhanded compliment about French "atmospheric railways" from the *New York Tribune*: "It is so rare to meet with anything in these old countries in advance of America in real, practical utility—in the inventive genius which has an utilitarian end—that we have deemed a short description of this most admirable and really interesting invention might prove acceptable to our readers."[65]

The same Paris correspondent who had so clearly supported the colonization of Algeria, in the same 1845 letter wrote about the spread of railways in terms of the "advancement of the arts": "Not only England, but Europe will speedily be spread over with a network of these powerful agents of intercommunication. When that is accomplished, what autocrat can check the diffusion of knowledge, and the consequent dissemination of liberal political ideas?"[66] "B.H.R.," reporting from Paris in 1852, wrote a forceful attack on a French journalist who was "one of the pets of the Prince [Louis Napoleon]": "It is certain that if M. De Cassagnac was shot, no one would regard him, for he is the most peevish and despicable barking dog that ever lived." The correspondent also devoted much of his column to the new regulations against the press that had been promulgated in Vienna.[67]

In more frequent discursive struggle, understanding of a foreign culture was opposed with negative stereotypes (either ethnic or racial) about it. Discourse thus constructed is often striking in the evident incongruence between the writer's experience abroad and his cultural assumptions that are contradicted by the experience. Interestingly, this contradictory construction appears in correspondence from Italy for all three New York dailies, perhaps because of the importance of Italy in 1859 news due to the war and perhaps also because of the negative Anglo-Saxon stereotype of Latin races.

A *New York Times* correspondent commented that one needs ac-
quaintance with "that vivacious people" to understand that their "perfect indifference" to the injustices of the "Papal hierarchy" reveals no
lack of character, but rather they bear it as "an inevitable nuisance imposed on them for the imaginary benefit of the Christian world."[68] The
Times correspondent from Milan wrote admiringly (if not without an
initial hint of sarcasm) of the courage of Italian volunteers under Garibaldi; after a tongue-in-cheek explanation of how conscripted men
used to conjure all sorts of ailments to be excused from service, he
wrote:

Now all is changed. . . . The words "*abile*," "*buono*," (able or good for service)
falling from the surgeon's lips are received by the bystanders with acclamations
of joy. Mothers, sisters, and young brides who used to form a sort of funeral
procession as if following their loved ones to the grave, now hear them sen-
tenced to a far more dangerous service (for Garibaldi's camp may be regarded
as the Austrian target) not merely with calmness but with triumphant joy.[69]

The same, or another, *Times* writer in Turin, after arguing that the
battles in Italy were the Italians' fault (a debatable concept since they
were fighting Austrian occupation), nevertheless wrote movingly
about the human cost of one of the bloodiest battles, Magenta: "There
was one other work, however, which assured me that the destruction of
human life at Magenta had not been over-estimated. In very many
places the ground was red."[70]

The Venice correspondent for the *New York Herald* seemed caught
between condescension and admiration for the stereotypical Italian
trait of the ability to enjoy life and art, especially when the Venetians
were proving that trait under the threat of war:

Even the prospect of war does not have the effect to diminish the desire for
pleasure among the Venetians, and I verily believe if a French fleet should drop
in here some fine night, and commence showering shell into Venice, the [Car-
nival] masqueraders would continue dancing to the music of the flying shot
and tumbling structures. . . . Truly it is to be hoped for the sake of art that there
will be no war in Italy; and the love of art is so joined with the love of life and
even liberty in the Italian people, that this feeling, doubtless, has a great effect
upon them in restraining them from revolution.[71]

Perhaps the best embodiment of this dichotomous construction of
Italians was found in the *New York Tribune* Turin correspondence from
July 1859. The writer inspected the part of Piedmont that had been

freed from the Austrians and found it desolated. In a striking example of balanced reporting, he declared he had confirmed the accounts of Austrian misconduct by interviewing Austrian prisoners. The Italians, however, were taking the devastating occupation philosophically—and the writer professed to admire, yet be astonished by, this show of equanimity that was just not like them:

The impression left upon my mind by a two days' ride through this scene of desolation will be strong enough to last me all my lifetime. . . . [E]very trace of cultivation had almost entirely disappeared. In many localities the former surface of the country has been entirely changed by the leveling of rising grounds, and the erection of artificial hights [*sic*]; but everywhere, every vestige of vegetation had been destroyed, and where your eye was once greeted by the fresh green of the meadows, by waving rice and wheat fields, by the vine clustering round the mulberry tree, it meets now with nothing but the dreary gray of the naked, hard-stamped earth, fields laid waste, and the stiff rectangular forms of the bulwarks, with not vegetation enough to feed even a goat—in short, a scene that reminded me of the excavated cities of the dead, in the East. . . . I was very much astonished at finding the inhabitants in a state of stupefied resignation to their fate, where I had expected the rage of despair. . . . Communicative as the Italians generally are, I met with little disposition on their part to converse on the visitation which had been inflicted upon them; but in all those instances in which I could overcome their moody reserve and get them to speak, they descanted on their misfortunes with *an enviable philosophical equanimity . . . I could not help admiring the good common sense and stoical fortitude of mind with which these—generally very ignorant—people appreciated the conduct and discussed the merits of their spoilers.*[72] [italics added]

If correspondents from Italy had difficulty in reconciling their stereotypes about Italians with the reality they met abroad and with their personal sympathy for the people, their colleagues experienced similar struggles while writing about one of the most culturally ostracized ethnicities in nineteenth-century America—the free blacks in the Caribbean islands. That a contradictory construction would exist for that population and in that location is per se a sign of the powerfulness of the foreign experience for correspondents. In the discursive context of Manifest Destiny, so often accompanied by Anglo-Saxon superiority, it is surprising to find not stereotypes but challenges to them in the correspondence. Both examples found of these particular contradictory constructions were written by correspondents of the *New York Times*.

"Robur's" letters in 1852 from Port-au-Prince, Haiti, carefully described the local scenery, including the "sad" spectacle of abandoned plantations where "frightened lizards daily sun themselves on the threshold";[73] he criticized the inhabitants' supposed laziness, and yet found ample justification for it:

If the people of this Island would only *work*, they might maintain a just claim to the title which they still fondly bestow upon their beloved Hayti [*sic*], "Queen of the Antilles." But they have struggled so hard and so valiantly for *liberty*, and feel so keenly the degraded estimation in which they are held by many of their fellow men, to whom God has given a lighter skin, and reminded, as they constantly are, that a sister Island within sixty miles of their shore, holds thousands and hundreds of thousands of their brethren, still in bondage, it is not strange, perhaps, that they should be slow to beat their swords into plough shares and their spears into pruning hooks.[74]

The 1859 letter from "W.G.S.," a *Times* "special correspondent" to Bridgetown, Barbados, is quoted at length below to illustrate how blatant both constructions are within the contradictory discourse:

No greater contrast could possibly be imagined than that between New York, in the month of January, and this beautiful Barbadoes [*sic*] . . .—a *seductive goddess* of the deep just risen from her couch and lying *voluptuously* in Old Neptune's lap. . . . There lay the island, bathed in the rich light of a tropic evening. The sun, fast sinking in the opposite horizon, was dripping with liquid gold. . . . It was but a bank of gently sloping verdure as *compared with our extended landscape views*—but so *deliciously soft*, so fresh, so fair, so varied in its minute scenery and in its shade and coloring, that the eye would *feast itself* with the sight only to turn and feast itself again. . . . I was soon sensible that prejudice done prevented me from regarding these people as quite equal, in what a Yankee would call smartness, to those of their own standing in any large American or European city. . . . *As an American, with all the prejudices of an American (if you choose to call them so) against the African race, I feel rebuked* as I move here along their dwellings. Humble as they are, the very worst locality that can be selected in Bridgetown is clean, and offers a great contrast to a New York Mulberry Street. . . . Loyal to the Government of the Great Empire which could afford to pour out gold like water and desolate some of its fairest provinces in order to unloose bonds which the slaves themselves scarcely felt, and from which, at first, they had no desire to be released . . . the Barbadian negro . . . boasts, *with all the pride of a down-East Yankee*, that he is free.[75] [italics added]

The contradictions in that article are quite extraordinary. The writer began his correspondence with a construction of Barbados that is at once racist, sexist, and imperialist. Describing the non-Western world as a female body is one of the topoi of imperialistic discourse and here the correspondent described the island as a voluptuous goddess, alluring, to be feasted upon by the white visitor.[76] Just a few lines after that, he acknowledged his racial prejudice and wrote about the change in perception and perspective he experienced after visiting the island and seeing how its people lived. Three times he compared the free Barbados blacks with white Americans and put them on the level of equality, first only within the same socioeconomic level ("to those of their own standing"), then generally for their common pride in asserting their freedom ("with all the pride of a down-East Yankee"). There is perhaps no better proof of the pervasiveness and lack of self-consciousness of a commonsense discourse than the fact that this correspondent could write in the same article (one assumes unconsciously) within the parameters of the "beautiful savage" type of colonialist discourse and also denounce the "prejudices" that underlie precisely that discourse. The contradiction also suggests the role foreign experience may play in the correspondents' modifying the developing discourses of the "world."

Ambivalent, contradictory constructions are also a sign of the evolution of American foreign correspondence across the first two decades of its existence. Indeed, their presence represents the biggest change between the earliest correspondence read in the late 1830s and the latest read from 1859. The format of early correspondence tended to parallel the travel letter, while later correspondence was written more often as political and social analysis; nevertheless, the two types coexisted throughout the period studied. Among constructions present throughout the two decades were those of American superiority to the rest of the "world" and the related discourse of Manifest Destiny and mission.

By 1852, however, the germ of a potential paradigm shift was present in the correspondence; all examples of correspondence critical of the discourse of superiority and of U.S. foreign policy were found in 1852 and 1859. The ambivalent coexistence of superiority/sympathy and of stereotypes irreconcilable with experience abroad also dates from 1852.

Several explanations are reasonable for the emergence of new constructions of foreign cultures. Since organized foreign correspondence had existed for nearly fifteen years and several correspondents in 1859 had been abroad for a few years, it is likely that understanding of foreign cultures was increasing proportionately to familiarity with those cultures. Also, as noted both in this chapter and in Chapter 3, correspondents and editors showed increasing concern about standards of truthfulness, accuracy, and balance, and this may have made them more critical of their reporting and aware of their own assumptions. Finally, the *New York Times* in the 1850s was quickly becoming a leader in foreign news and correspondence, in quality if not in quantity (which was still less than that in the *New York Herald*); and the correspondents for the newspaper, as noted in the examples above, were particularly critical of U.S. foreign policy and often ambivalent about foreign realities both along with, and in contradiction to, the themes of American superiority and mission.

Of the constructions that remained prevalent in selected newspapers studied at intervals across the years from 1838 through 1859, the most prominent was the comparison of foreign cultures (and whatever product thereof) with the United States, usually favorable to the American counterpart. While such construction is a rather natural result of the creation of common sense for literally foreign realities, it also implicitly reinforces the discourse of the "world's" inferiority to the United States. Correspondence was often condescending, ridiculing, or overtly caustic about the inability of foreign leaders (and sometimes entire populations) to rise to the American level of democratic enlightenment or economic prosperity. While this construction conforms to the discourse of American mission and Manifest Destiny, only the *New York Herald* correspondents wrote explicitly supporting annexation. (The editorials in that paper were also the most supportive of territorial acquisition, as noted in the previous chapter.).

The themes of Manifest Destiny surrounding the issues of annexation and of American superiority in terms of foreign threats to either the safety or the international reputation and power of the United States are significantly less prominent in correspondence than in foreign policy debates and editorials. This suggests a certain freedom on the part of correspondents from the governmental establishment and from their own newspapers' editorial courses. In newspapers of the 1850s, contradictory constructions were found that were either critical of the American approach to foreign cultures or openly empathetic to the foreign countries. In several articles, the correspondents appeared to struggle with reconciling stereotypes (be it "vivacious" Italians or "voluptuous" Caribbean islands) with the realities they witnessed abroad.

Some writers expressed this struggle by declaring themselves surprised at their (almost subconscious) admiration for foreign cultures. That they should feel conflict about their assumptions (and stereotypes) can be interpreted as a sign that the discourse of the "world" was evolving toward a construction of foreign realities based more on their own merits than on their supposed inferiority to the United States. That a contradictory discourse including alternative constructions of the "world" should be found in correspondence rather than in editorials or policy discussions seems to indicate that Americans reporting from abroad did make a difference in how foreign cultures were constructed in the newspapers. Whether women correspondents for mainstream newspapers and correspondents for a black newspaper constructed yet more alternative meanings about the "world" is the subject of Chapter 6.

NOTES

1. See *New York Tribune*, November 5, 1852, p. 6. A *New York Herald* Paris correspondent parodied the lack of foreign language skills of American and British travelers, writing that translations are "a glorious provision of nature, or the lexicographers, or of whoever had the management of the matter" and that English-speaking people in Paris had the same "delightful feeling" upon seeing the words "English Spoken" in a restaurant "that a thirsty traveller in the Arabian deserts may be supposed to have when his eyes first light upon a well of sparkling water"; November 3, 1859, p. 2.

2. *New York Tribune*, November 4, 1852, p. 6.

3. Spurr also emphasizes literary journalism in his study of colonial discourse; he justifies his choice by stressing the "metonymic and historically referential" qualities of the genre; David Spurr, *The Rhetoric of Empire* (Durham, N.C.: Duke University Press, 1993): 3–8.

4. "[I] was compensated for the discomfort of the dust by the satisfaction I felt at the explosion of the superstition that the New York Central Railway enjoys a monopoly in that commodity," *Boston Transcript*, July 8, 1859, p. 2; *New York Herald*, July 21, 1838, p. 2 (Bennett maintained that rain showers in the United States are longer because everything there is bigger).

5. *New York Times*, July 8, 1859, p. 1; *Charleston Courier*, November 1, 1838, p. 2.

6. *New York Herald*, July 23, 1838, p. 2; July 17, 1838, p. 2.

7. *New York Herald*, September 1, 1859, p. 1 and September 2, 1859, p. 1; the Florence correspondent added in the same article that the election to the Tuscan Assembly had been "conducted with so much regularity and good order as to be a model for countries having a larger experience of the elective privilege."

8. *New York Herald*, September 2, 1859, p. 1; also, in the same paper, Bennett's letter, July 30, 1838, p. 2: "All English people of any leisure have been on the Continent, they possess a taste which would put our fashionables in New York entirely in the back ground [*sic*]. Indeed the more I see of soci-

ety here, the more laughable does the pretended fashionable of New York seem to be."

9. *New York Tribune*, November 5, 1852, p. 5; December 2, 1845, p. 1. An editorial in the *New York Herald* chastised American art buyers for acquiring any foreign object just because it was foreign, not because of its artistic merits, thus closing the market to American artists: "It suffices us that the European critics have stamped their approbation on the works of an artist, for his worst productions, or even imitations of them, to be preferred to the most meritorious compositions of our own printers. . . . This is not the way to encourage art in this country"; *New York Herald*, November 4, 1852, p. 4.

10. *New York Herald*, July 18, 1838, p. 2.

11. *Chicago Tribune*, November 10, 1853, p. 2; signed William B. Ogden.

12. *New York Times*, July 20, 1852, p. 1 and July 27, 1852, p. 1.

13. *New York Herald*, July 21, 1838, p. 2. Similarly, "D.D.M.," *Missouri Republican* correspondent in England, called Great Britain "this wonderful little island," adding "England is five hundred years in advance of the United States in some things, and about as much behind her in some others"; September 1, 1859, p. 2.

14. *New York Herald*, September 2, 1859, p. 1.

15. *New York Tribune*, January 6, 1859, p. 3 and November 7, 1859, p. 6 (European powers convened at Zurich after the Italian war). Also, *New York Times*, December 3, 1852, p. 3, signed "Aletheiologos": "We have not yet, it would seem, come to the last *monomania* of Irish politics. . . . Once the changes in progress are completed . . . Ireland will no longer be a bye-word among the nations."

16. *New York Tribune*, September 2, 1859, p. 6. The following excerpt from the Paris correspondence of *Washington Republic* is also illustrative of this kind of ridicule: "Not all the police of Paris could keep order at the barriers on Sunday, if the little green tables, and the beer and the fried potatoes, and the blue wine were put under lock and key. . . . I firmly believe that a Sunday law passed just now, at the commencement of summer, would not only lead to bloodshed, but would produce a revolution that would overthrow the government." Reprinted in the *Boston Transcript*, July 1, 1852, p. 2.

17. *New York Times*, July 8, 1859, p. 2. The *New York Herald* Venetian correspondent wrote that Italians usually harbored "wild, impracticable schemes," March 3, 1859, p. 2.

18. *New York Herald*, September 2, 1859, p. 1.

19. Turin correspondence, *New York Tribune*, July 8, 1859, p. 6 and London correspondence, same paper, November 7, 1859, p. 6.

20. *New York Tribune*, March 4, 1852, p. 6; *New York Tribune*, November 5, 1852, p. 6.

21. *New York Herald*, December 3, 1838, p. 2. Also, *New York Tribune*, September 2, 1852, p. 5; correspondence from Argentina: "Thus these beautiful countries, which have been for ten years lacerated by internal discord and war, appear to be no nearer to the enjoyment of peace and liberty." Incidentally, even Europe, not the locus of interventionist aims, was constructed mostly in terms of unsettled strife: "Believe me, the affairs of Europe are still in a very ticklish state," *New York Herald*, July 2, 1852, p. 2.

22. *New York Times*, July 19, 1852, p. 1.

23. *New York Times*, July 19, 1852, p. 1.

24. *New York Times*, January 6, 1859, p. 2; the writer introduced the statement above by saying, "I could not help drawing the contrast between the darkness and civilization to be encountered in this beautiful valley."

25. *Charleston Courier* Havana correspondence, September 2, 1859, p. 2.

26. *New York Herald*, July 8, 1859, p. 1.

27. That statement was prefaced by this chillingly imperialistic argument by the same Paris correspondent: "It is an ungrateful duty for the armies of civilised [*sic*] nations to have to contend with savage tribes," *New York Herald*, November 6, 1845, p. 1.

28. *New York Tribune*, March 4, 1852, p. 6.

29. *New York Herald*, March 5, 1852, p. 3.

30. *New York Herald*, May 5, 1859, p. 1.

31. *New York Herald*, September 2, 1859, p. 8.

32. *New York Herald*, September 1, 1859, p. 1.

33. Reprinted in the *Boston Transcript*, January 6, 1859, p. 1.

34. *New York Herald*, January 7, 1859, p. 3; July 7, 1859, p. 1; November 3, 1859, p. 5.

35. *New York Herald*, September 3, 1852, p. 2.

36. *New York Tribune*, January 6, 1859, p. 3.

37. *New York Herald*, September 3, 1852, p. 2.

38. *New York Herald*, January 6, 1859, p. 8. The writer added, condescendingly, "as customary during the Christmas holidays, several persons have been stabbed in our streets." "Occatur," *New York Times* correspondent from Havana, while not in favor of armed intervention, still wrote that "national equity" "has been lost sight of on the east side of the Atlantic," December 7, 1852, p. 6.

39. *New Orleans Picayune*, May 2, 1845, p. 2.

40. *New York Herald*, September 3, 1852, p. 2.

41. *New York Times*, January 6, 1859, p. 2.

42. *New York Times*, November 4, 1859, p. 2.

43. *New York Herald*, July 17, 1838, p. 2 and July 30, 1838, p. 2. Also, July 27, 1838, p. 2: "The popularity of the American republic with the British government is singularly strong and marked."

44. *New York Times*, July 27, 1852, p. 1.

45. *New York Herald*, September 1, 1859, p. 1.

46. *New York Herald*, September 2, 1859, p. 2.

47. *New Orleans Picayune*, November 6, 1859, p. 1.

48. *New York Times*, September 2, 1859, p. 1, signed "Adios."

49. *New York Tribune*, November 7, 1859, p. 6.

50. *Boston Transcript*, July 8, 1859, p. 2.

51. *New York Times*, July 8, 1859, p. 1.

52. Michael Schudson, *Discovering the News* (New York: Basic Books, 1978): 147.

53. "[The] Germans have directed their most constant and persevering efforts to the conquest, colonization, or at least civilization, of the East of Europe"; *New York Tribune*, March 5, 1852, p. 7.

54. *New York Herald*, May 6, 1852, p. 7. Another in-depth foreign analysis can be read in the *New York Tribune* Toronto correspondence, May 5, 1859, p. 6.

55. *Missouri Republican*, September 2, 1852, p. 2 and September 1, 1859, p. 2.

56. *Charleston Courier*, March 3, 1859, p. 1.

57. *New York Times*, May 6, 1859, p. 1.

58. *New York Times*, July 8, 1859, p. 1.

59. *New York Times*, September 1, 1859, p. 1.

60. *New York Herald*, July 8, 1859, p. 1; September 2, 1859, p. 2.

61. *New York Times*, July 20, 1852, p. 1.

62. *New York Tribune*, November 4, 1852, p. 6.

63. *New York Tribune*, March 4, 1852, p. 6.

64. *New York Tribune*, November 5, 1852, p. 6.

65. Paris correspondence for *The Ohio State Journal*, reprinted in the *New York Tribune*, November 4, 1852, p. 5.

66. *New York Herald*, November 6, 1845, p. 1.

67. *New York Herald*, July 2, 1852, p. 2.

68. *New York Times*, November 3, 1859, p. 2.

69. In his letter, incidentally, is one of the very rare instances of interviews in American antebellum journalism; the correspondent interviewed several wounded volunteers at a camp near Milan and then wrote an account of Garibaldi's latest campaign, incorporating some of their direct quotes ("It was as if we had been shooting hares," said one of their number to me. "'There are two skulking behind the hedge.' 'Fire on that chap to the left of the tree.' 'There's one to your right.' Such were the constant warnings we gave each other as we stopped to reload our guns."); *New York Times*, July 8, 1859, p. 1.

70. *New York Times*, July 8, 1859, p. 2.

71. *New York Herald*, March 3, 1859, p. 2.

72. *New York Tribune*, July 8, 1859, p. 6.

73. *New York Times*, July 28, 1852, p. 3.

74. *New York Times*, December 10, 1852, p.2.

75. *New York Times*, March 4, 1859, p. 8.

76. See Spurr's chapter on "Eroticization," pp. 170–183.

CHAPTER 6

ALTERNATIVE CONSTRUCTIONS OF THE "WORLD"

One of the assumptions of this book was that women writers and correspondents for the black press could have given the world meanings alternative to those constructed by their white, male colleagues working for mainstream newspapers, as discussed in the previous chapter. They did, but because of different, more negative perceptions of the United States, rather than different, more sympathetic understandings of foreign countries.

The study of correspondence by selected women writers and by the correspondents for a black newspaper reveals that some of the constructions of the "world" found in women's writings, as well as in the correspondence published in the black paper selected, are identical to those found in editorials and correspondence in mainstream newspapers. Especially prominent is the discourse of American superiority and mission. However, these writers' experiences as minorities in the United States seem to have led them to qualify the discourse of American superiority—not because they found it irreconcilable with foreign reality, but because they could not embrace the role of the United States as light to the world's downtrodden peoples when American women and blacks were oppressed. Therefore, some of the writings of the correspondents discussed in this chapter are sites of struggle, but between contradictory constructions of America, rather than of foreign cultures.

Between 1838 and 1859, mainstream journalism—represented by the newspapers and the editors discussed in Chapters 4 and 5—systematically excluded two groups of Americans, women and blacks. There were a few notable exceptions of women on the staffs of mainstream papers in positions ranging from editors to reporters; and, of course, there was a growing black press. But for the most part, women journalists were limited to "appropriate" subjects, likely to occupy "home department" columns, or, increasingly in the 1850s, to women's rights publications. Similarly, black journalists wrote almost exclusively for black newspapers or for the abolitionist press. But women were also engaged to write foreign correspondence. As Julia Edwards noted, until the 1870s, women could travel to Europe and report from there for the same editors who would not hire them as reporters in their hometowns.[1] And at least some black newspapers had columns of foreign news and correspondence.

The purpose of this chapter is to discuss the writings of three women foreign correspondents and those of the anonymous foreign correspondents for a black newspaper, the *North Star*, and to identify constructions of the "world" and whether (and how) those differed from the constructions in the mainstream press discussed in the previous chapter. While it is assumed that gender and race may influence discursive practices and the construction of reality, it falls outside the scope of this study to examine the merits of this assumption. What is significant to this study is that constructions of foreign cultures by writers with perspectives different from those of the vast majority of antebellum American journalists could suggest both the pervasiveness of the discourses found in mainstream newspapers and the existence of alternative constructions.

For consistency's sake, since the correspondence cited in the previous chapter was written both by famous figures like Bayard Taylor and by journalists whose very identity is unknown, it was deemed important to include in this section the writings of famous writers like Margaret Fuller and of much less known women correspondents (like Sara Jane Clarke) or those whose correspondence has never been studied or even collected (like Nancy Johnson).

Just as the constructions of foreign correspondence discussed in Chapter 5 cannot be taken to represent the views of the "world" held by the public in the antebellum United States, the constructions found in correspondence discussed in this chapter are not assumed to be representatives of what contemporary women and blacks thought of foreign cultures. But if the discourse in foreign correspondence helped create an American commonsense view of the "world," then it bears investigating whether correspondents belonging to then-marginalized groups constructed foreign cultures within the same discourse or in ambivalent constructions.

CONSTRUCTIONS OF THE "WORLD" IN WOMEN CORRESPONDENTS' WRITINGS

Women started entering the field of journalism in significant numbers only in the last two decades of the nineteenth century.[2] Until then, there were few women involved in either publishing, editing, or writing for mainstream newspapers. During the late eighteenth and early nineteenth centuries, women editors and publishers usually assumed those duties to sustain the family business when the male members of the family had either temporarily left or died.[3] In the nineteenth century, the rowdy realm of party and penny papers was considered unladylike and women were usually kept out of newsrooms. Fuller was one of the first women on staff at a major newspaper when Horace Greeley hired her in 1844. Even at the *New York Tribune*, Fuller did not completely defy conventions, for she started as literary critic and did most of her writing at Greeley's home. In fact, it was much more usual for women to sell their writings, either poetry or human interest prose, to newspapers than be employed as reporters.[4]

Being denied full access to the supposedly free "marketplace of ideas" of the nineteenth-century press, several women, much like blacks and reformers, started their own periodicals.[5] By 1850, twenty-five publications were edited by women; most of those periodicals, like *Godey's Lady's Book*, reinforced the cultural myths of womanhood and domesticity, while a few publications were the mouthpieces of the growing women's rights movement and other reforms.[6]

The three women correspondents whose writings are discussed here, then, represent exceptions. Fuller was probably the first woman foreign correspondent when Greeley sent her to Europe in the summer of 1846; between then and January 1850 she wrote thirty-seven dispatches for the *New York Tribune* from Great Britain, France, and Italy. Between 1848–1850, Fuller resided in Italy, where she witnessed (and participated in) the Roman revolution against the Pope and the French; she married a Roman nobleman and had a son, but the three died in a shipwreck in 1850 on the return trip to the United States.

Sara Jane Clarke Lippincott, writing under the pen name of Grace Greenwood, became the second woman Washington correspondent in

1850, writing for the antislavery paper, the *National Era*, and the *Saturday Evening Post* of Philadelphia.[7] For the same two publications, she wrote from Europe in 1852–1853; in 1870 she was again in Washington, corresponding for the *New York Tribune* and the *New York Times*.[8] Nancy Johnson, also known as Anna Cummings Johnson or Minnie Myrtle, wrote European correspondence for the *New York Times* beginning in 1857; her pioneering journalistic efforts are all the more striking because she had lost a leg in her youth.[9]

The question of whether women foreign correspondents view the "world" with different eyes from their male colleagues has been discussed by scholars and by the journalists themselves.[10] Several scholars have examined the relationship between nineteenth-century travel writing (including foreign correspondence) and gender from the perspective of the construction of particular discourses. Stowe has argued that European travel helped nineteenth-century Americans construct their identity as Americans first, and then along definitions of class, race, and gender, for which they could gain added respectability just by traveling.[11] Foster, studying specifically women travelers and writers, has argued that there is a "distinctive and feminine voice in the women's texts, ways of seeing and recreating foreign experience which are clearly gender-related." She also found that women writers tended to relate more sympathetically to foreigners than did male writers, who were in turn more likely to be aggressive in constructing the "other" in an object position.[12]

Schriber, who examined the writings of American women abroad from the 1830s to the early twentieth century, concluded that everything in the writers' world "was charged with gender ideology."[13] Of particular relevance to this study of discourse in foreign correspondence is her argument that writers constructed foreign cultures differently, depending on their gender, because gender informed the discourse of American mission. In fact, Schriber argues that, since Woman was seen as the symbol of (American) republican virtue, she was also the symbol of the destiny of progress and therefore culturally constructed as twice superior, to American men and to foreign women.

Schriber also found that women travel writers rarely challenged the myth of American exceptionalism, and therefore their texts "are often arms of nationalism, classism, racism, the practice of 'othering,' and patriarchal definitions of Woman."[14] Therefore, Schriber concluded, travel texts are quite similar regardless of the author's gender; perhaps the most significant discursive gender difference is that women are even stronger followers of the American superiority discourse: "The once-colonized American now insists on the superiority of the United States even while, ironically, worshipping at historic shrines abroad in a massive effort at appropriation. In the instance of the female traveler, a sense of national superiority is further inflated by a sense of gender superiority."[15]

The constructions of the "world" in the writings of Greenwood, Johnson, and Fuller show that Schriber's argument is valid only to a certain degree, for Johnson and Fuller reveal significant, albeit different, discursive contradictions. Of the three, Greenwood's work was definitely the most in line with the genre of travel writing and her constructions are rather constricted by a "guidebook" approach to her European travels. Her travel correspondence was collected in an 1854 book, *Haps and Mishaps of a Tour in Europe*, which was very popular and remained in print for nearly half a century.[16]

Her first letter, dated Liverpool, June 10, 1853, describes the voyage to Europe and the "depths of dread" she felt upon sailing from New York for the unknown—a conventional beginning, but not an auspicious one for a sympathetic understanding of foreign cultures.[17] Her first impressions of Europe oscillate between gushing admiration for the green shores of Ireland and ridicule for the facilities of Liverpool that could not compete with the greatly superior ones in the United States: "Liverpool first struck me as differing from our seaport towns, in having a vastly greater number of docks, vessels, police officers, ragged boys, red-faced men, barefooted women, and donkey carts."[18] A September letter lists with conventional poeticism the natural and historical sights in the Irish countryside. A December letter from Rome, describing some of the sights but also a Franciscan procession for a religious holiday, reveals not only the strength of prejudices in Greenwood's understanding of foreign cultures (particularly anti-Latin and anti-Catholic stereotypes), but also a rather imperialist "gaze" on her part. She defined the Franciscans as the "ugliest, coarsest, and most animal-looking set of men" she ever saw; describing the "bewildering" eyes of peasants on Rome's streets, she said she could not help but "behold them with an ever-unsatisfied interest"—a different construction of the gaze only in that the gazer is a woman.[19]

A later letter from Milan and her last dispatch from London are slightly more sympathetic to the local people. Writing from Milan, Greenwood expressed admiration for the conduct of the population under the despotic Austrian rule. She also wrote admiringly of the parks and walks around the city, which were absent from American cities—but then, just like Ogden of the *Chicago Tribune*, Greenwood attributed the beautification of foreign cities to their despotic governments, again implicitly reinforcing the concept of American superiority, since a free government likely offset the disadvantage of architectural gloom.[20] Finally, in her letter from London, Greenwood gushed about her meetings with the revolutionary exiles Louis Kossuth and Giuseppe Mazzini. The former impressed her with the "almost superhuman power of his presence," the latter with his eyes' "wonderful outlooking of power and destiny"; in this, Greenwood added, Mazzini's eyes are different from "most Italian eyes," which bespeak either "despairing indolence" or "slumberous passion."[21]

With the exception of the fact that it is a woman who is observing foreign cultures, Greenwood's correspondence remains within the boundaries of a discourse of American superiority. The writings by Johnson and Fuller are much more ambivalent. Either their sense of America or their sense of the "world" seems to contradict a sense of American superiority. Johnson, who wrote in *Myrtle Wreath* that a woman's mission was "to impress the heart, and to amuse," wrote in her European correspondence about gender-relevant topics, like tea parties and women's labor, but she seems to have been influenced by some feminist thought.[22]

In her second letter from Germany, she wrote about her goal in making the trip: "To study the people of these old fogy, yet restless and turbulent principalities, which are pouring forth every year their myriads upon our shores."[23] The sentence is revealing of her approach to Europe—she constructed it as old (clearly compared to the United States), rife with conflict, and especially important because of its relationship (immigration) with America. In her very first letter, after describing the ship's departure much along the lines used by Greenwood, Johnson thus stamped her first experience of the British shore: "This is not Yankee land."[24] One of the dominant characteristics of this "unAmericanism" was, in Johnson's view, the Germans' slowness in becoming "modified and modernized," that is, more like the British and the Americans: "Germans are so slow in running after new things that what is old retains deep root in their hearts long after they are convinced that something else is better."[25] Johnson's writings about Europe were also strongly influenced by class; she once rode in the third-class cart of a train to see "the vulgar" and labeled the people living in the German countryside as "entirely without culture or polish."[26] Incidentally, all three women correspondents studied exhibited a strong class prejudice, definitely stronger than observed in the writings by the correspondents examined in Chapter 5. A possible explanation is that women who could travel to Europe and write for newspapers in the mid-nineteenth century were most likely of the upper echelons of society, while male journalists came from more varied backgrounds.

Although she approached Europe with class prejudices and a sense of American progress, Johnson also wrote sympathetically of the condition of European women, as well as ambivalently about the prejudices of Americans abroad. Johnson twisted the construction of bad governments ruining their own people, noted in the previous chapter, into the following critique, which must have resonated with her female American readers:

The [German] men are all required for soldiers, and dressed in gay uniforms, are practicing military tactics, or idling away their time in barracks. We have often seen it alluded to as an evidence of oppression and cruelty, that women perform the labor of men [in the fields]. To work in the sun makes them look coarse, but the labor itself is not more exhausting than many kinds which belong exclusively to the house. To wash and iron and cook, day after day, is considered womanly employment, but compared with it, digging and hoeing are trifling affairs.[27]

In the following letter, Johnson compared the freedom of movement of European women to the American convention that proper ladies alone should travel only escorted by a married couple, and concluded: "Barriers and conventionalisms are very important, we suppose, to well-regulated society, but in our somewhat extensive observations we are quite surprised to see of how little use they are for their ostensible purposes. Where there is a will there is a way in moral as well as in mental and physical difficulties. Those careful parents who hesitate to bring their children to Europe lest they be demoralized, might sometimes find it well to be careful that they do not come to demoralize Europe."[28]

Such a construction contradicted the discourse of American superiority. But it seems attributable to the fact that Johnson found American superiority hard to reconcile with her reality as a woman in the United States and not because, like some of her fellow correspondents, she found the concept irreconcilable with the observed foreign reality. Fuller also wrote ambivalently of foreign realities, especially because she increasingly identified with the foreign people she wrote about. Writing about Americans abroad in one of her dispatches, Fuller criticized their prejudices against Italians, especially the view (observed in some editorials in Chapter 4) that people degraded by bad governments were not worthy of better ones; she also said that the best type of traveling American was the one who earnestly sought to learn from "the seed of the past." Nevertheless, this "thinking American," Fuller wrote, "recognizes the immense advantage of being born to a new world and on a virgin soil."[29] This kind of contradiction—foreign peoples deserve better understanding from Americans because they can then be helped by the Americans' light—betrays the discourse of mission and criticism to it, both of which imbued Fuller's correspondence.

Of the three women correspondents discussed here, Fuller wrote the most political and analytical correspondence, in line not so much with travel letter writing but with the work of her male colleagues in other European capitals.[30] Her writing also showed the most sympathy for foreign cultures, especially her homeland elect, Italy. Still, from her dispatches, it seems that she thought her best means to forward the Italian revolutionary cause, which she full-heartedly supported, was to inform, and rally the support of, the American people. Simply put, even when she criticized her homeland for lack of knowledge or leadership, she still believed in America's mission to advance progress in the world, however disinterestedly. Schriber has argued that, by the very will to shape American public opinion, Fuller was operating within the broad discourse of American interests.[31] The same, paradoxically, can be said about Roberts' argument that Fuller sought to use Europe to redeem the United States and incite Americans to overcome their faults. In fact, even in this guise, this is still a discourse about American republicanism.[32]

Fuller traveled to Europe in 1846 at a time of great social and political upheavals; by 1848–1849 there were general discontent, labor unrest, and spreading socialist ideals that erupted in outright revolutions from Naples to Vienna. When Fuller arrived in 1847, Italy was not a united nation, and Rome was part of the Papal states, ruled by Pius IX; by 1850, when she sailed to the United States, Rome had experienced a revolutionary republican government and then a bombardment as the French laid siege to the city and succeeded in restoring the exiled pope's rule, despite Mazzini's desperate resistance. During those years, Fuller grew more radical in her socialist thinking and more convinced that the struggle she was witnessing in Italy embodied a sweeping historical movement toward human freedom and equality.[33]

Her first dispatch from England in August 1846 starts with tales from the ocean crossing, without the kind of patriotic regrets for the disappearing U.S. shore expressed by Greenwood and Johnson. Fuller also quoted liberally from English and American literature.[34] A year

later, in an October 1847 letter from Rome, Fuller had switched entirely from the descriptive travel writer to the analytical observer. She
wrote of the Romans' hopeful expectations that Pius IX would begin a
reform, and the first steps toward republicanism recently taken in Florence.[35] Her construction of the Italian reforming effort is quite contradictory; she is passionate, yet condescending ("I saw with pleasure [the
Romans'] childlike joy and trust"); and even though she believes that
Italy can find "salvation" if free from foreign aid and aggression, she
considers Italians not quite civil ("they are wanted in the civilized world
as a peculiar influence"). Most significantly, Fuller wrote of the role of
Americans in the Florentine celebrations, saying not only that the spirit
animating Tuscany was that of the founding fathers, but also that her
compatriots had becomingly "erected the American Eagle where its cry
ought to be heard from afar, where a Nation is striving for independent
existence and a Government to represent the People." She concluded
her dispatch writing that America should express sympathy for Italy because, with all its "talent given," it had a "heavy account to render."
Appealing to fellow Americans to aid the European revolutions, she
wrote: "This cause is OURS, above all others"—a construction of the
Italian Risorgimento that is at once fully sympathetic and completely
within the discourse of American mission.

In two dispatches a year later, while Rome was under the republican
government, Fuller wrote much more militantly about the revolutionary cause, praising the Romans for their courage, coolness, and compo-
sure (as well as the "wild, innocent gayety of which this people alone is
capable after childhood") amidst assassinations and the pope's flight.
Still, she pleaded for a better American ambassador, "one that has experience of foreign life" (adding she might be a good candidate, but "another century") and wished to her country, "may she be worthy of the
privileges she possesses, while others are lavishing their blood to win
them."[36] This last sentence indicates a slight shift in Fuller's discourse
of American mission—the United States is still constructed as destined
to superior glory, but, it seems, through no particular effort on the
Americans' part.

Another year later, in the summer of 1849, when Fuller wrote about
Rome under siege, her marriage to the Italian cause was complete. She
wrote about the French attack as "miserable" and "especially barba-
rous," but futile because it only elicited "more and more courage" "*on
our side*," which is showing in thought and action a spirit "as ever animated the most precious facts we treasure from the heroic age"[37] [ital-
ics added]. In her second-to-last dispatch, in late 1849 from Florence,

she wrote despairingly of the state of failed revolutions throughout Italy and predicted that another "peaceful though radical revolution" would soon come, and governments would become socialist.[38] However radical such thinking must have seemed to her American readers, Fuller's writing continued to reflect the discourse of American mission. She wrote that Americans should not disdainfully forget that they owe their privileged status entirely to their free institutions, because by their bad deportment abroad they injure both America and the world: "America is the star of hope to the enslaved nations, bitter indeed were the night of the world if that star were hid from its sight by foul vapors."

Thus, the writings of the three women correspondents did not seriously challenge the discourse of the United States as the light to the world, the superior nation destined to lead the rest to freedom. Yet, the writings of Johnson and Fuller reflect alternatives to this construction: Fuller empathized with a foreign people at a higher level than other correspondents studied, making their cause her (and America's) cause; Johnson questioned the myth of American progress and freedom by focusing on the rigid conventions imposed on women.

Foreign correspondents for a black newspaper, as discussed below, constructed the "world" much as Johnson did. While a sense of America's superiority, or at least uniqueness, dominated their writings, they also found it rather irreconcilable with their experience in the largely racist United States.

CONSTRUCTIONS OF THE "WORLD" IN AN AFRICAN AMERICAN NEWSPAPER

By 1860, black journalists had established about forty newspapers, mostly dedicated to agitating for abolitionism and to sustaining the growing free black communities in the northern states.[39] The first black newspaper in the United States was *Freedom's Journal*, founded in 1827 in New York, which remained the center of black journalism throughout the antebellum period; only five publications were started in the South before 1865.[40] The newspapers were usually short-lived and financially unsuccessful; their pages were largely devoted to the cause of antislavery and the elevation of the black race, rather than general news, and their audiences were primarily abolitionists (black and white) in the North.[41]

The black newspaper with the largest circulation and the most influential presence on the scene of antebellum journalism was the *North Star*.[42] Frederick Douglass, a fugitive slave who had become an internationally renowned abolitionist lecturer and writer, founded the paper in November 1847 in Rochester, New York. The weekly *North Star* continued publishing until 1851, when Douglass merged it with another newspaper; the resulting paper, *Frederick Douglass' Paper*, ran through the 1850s. The *North Star* reached considerable circulation among white Americans, with a subscription list of 3,000 (the *Chicago Tribune*, which was then the most important newspaper in the Midwest, had only 4,000 circulation by 1857).[43]

Moreover, the *North Star* differed from contemporary black newspapers because Douglass established it not only to promote abolition, but also to prove that black journalism could be on a par with the white press.[44] The earliest historian of the black press wrote in 1891 that the *North Star* "was conducted on a much higher plane than any of the preceding publications. . . . [Douglass] demonstrated the fact that the Afro-American was equal to the white man in conducting a useful and popular journal."[45] He added that Douglass secured a corps of correspondents from Europe and the West Indies. Their writings are examined in this section.

A study of black editors' criticism of U.S. imperialism, albeit in the period of the Spanish-American war (1898–1900), found that "criticism of American wars against weaker nations has been an enduring black tradition."[46] The author argued that the tradition began with Douglass' criticism of the Mexican war in 1846, which is discussed below in the context of *North Star* editorials. But the relationship between antebellum black editors and the U.S. government (hence also its foreign policy) was particularly problematic, as black leaders disagreed on whether they should support a government that condoned slavery. Douglass condemned the U.S. Constitution but reversed that position in the early 1850s.[47]

One scholar who has written about black editors' attitudes toward American republicanism concluded that a "pro-American idealism" permeated the early black press.[48] She wrote that editors did not question the principles of the Revolution and American democratic ideals, but they believed that eventually white Americans would rise to those principles by including blacks—fascinatingly, much like Americans believed other nations could rise to their own republican level. According to Hutton, no early black editor was more supportive of American democracy than Douglass. The scholar argued, however, that this attitude did not mean slavishly following the principles of a largely racist people; it meant implicitly reminding Americans that those very principles were contradicted as long as blacks were enslaved.

Not surprisingly, then, the constructions of the "world" in the *North Star* were ambivalent as to the "mission" of the United States. Several editorials dealing with foreign matters were clearly critical of American policies; for example, one attacked the Mexican war, calling it "the result of long years of national transgression," and concluding that Americans had given themselves up "to the blind spirit of mad ambition."[49] In another, discussing the 1848 revolutions in France, the editor threateningly wrote: "We call upon tyrants the world over, and especially American tyrants, to look and reflect upon this late revolution in France."[50]

Foreign news and correspondence, however, in the *North Star* were remarkably similar to those in the mainstream newspapers discussed in Chapters 3 and 5. The first foreign news digest found was published on March 24, 1848, and it was indistinguishable from telegraph digests in newspapers like the *New Orleans Picayune* and the *New York Herald*. The only exception was the editor's preface to it: "Most of the readers of the *North Star* are doubtless already in possession of the very unexpected intelligence on Europe, and particularly French affairs, by the steamer Cambria. Still a brief statement of the most prominent facts may not be unacceptable." In fact, the editor must have deemed foreign digests very acceptable, because three and a half columns in the following issue were devoted to one. It started with briefs from Paris, such as, "The municipal guards are dissolved. The guard of the city of Paris is entrusted to the national guard, under the orders of M. Coutas, superior commandant of the national guard at Paris." This was followed by news from England, Ireland, Spain, Russia, Switzerland, Belgium, Austria, Prussia, Sicily, and Italy.[51] In January 1850, the digest of European news came via telegraph from Halifax, suggesting that it was either reprinted from another newspaper or bought from The Associated Press. Foreign news digests and foreign correspondence decreased throughout 1850 and 1851, ultimately leaning on topics primarily related to blacks or slavery.

The *North Star* foreign correspondence was also very similar to that in mainstream newspapers. Both the *North Star*'s and mainstream newspapers' foreign correspondents expressed concern about truthfulness, accuracy, and balance in their writings. "Harold," a correspondent from Haiti, promised at the end of his first letter that he would write again "in a short time—that is, when I have been here sufficiently long to render you *something like an impartial account* of matters and things so exceedingly novel"[52] [italics added]. "S.P.Q.R.," a London correspondent, also wrote about his concern that the public was becoming desensitized to news of violence, a very modern concern echoing that of the London correspondent for the *Boston Transcript* and the Italy correspondent for the *New York Times* discussed in the Chapter 3: "The man who, on perusing his morning paper, and finding it stated therein, that there had been a fall of one percent in the stocks, would have frightened his family with astonished exclamations, now reads, with the utmost unconcern, accounts of armed mob intervention—of an engagement involving the loss of thousands—of the flight of an emperor or the ruin of a dynasty."[53]

The style and format of foreign correspondence in the *North Star* also resembled those of mainstream newspapers. The earliest correspondence in the *North Star*, from London, merits quoting in its entirety as an example; especially noteworthy is that it started with a summary of trade and condescendingly constructed the abundance of bad news abroad, as some mainstream correspondents also did:

Trade continues exceedingly dull; and there is great distress and disease throughout the country. In London alone the deaths are more than double the usual average. In Ireland, there is murder among the rich, and death by famine among the poor, *as usual*. The Alliance [a male suffrage movement] is making progress; although, in consequence of our present commercial crisis, it is up-hill work. The cause of liberty and equality throughout the world, is destined ere long, to achieve a complete and final triumph. . . . We shall be glad to see your Star. . . . I am glad to hear of Garrison's recovery.[54] [italics added]

The letter, signed T.D., was followed by one signed R.D., detailing a political controversy over the appointment of the bishop of Hereford. For the first half of 1848, at least, "R.S.D." regularly sent correspondence of the analytical type from London, emphasizing business, politics, and the intricacies of revolutionary upheavals throughout Europe, which R.S.D. seemed to support. In his enthusiasm for the revolutions sweeping away European despotism and his penchant for business and coups, R.S.D. wrote correspondence that did not differ from that by his mainstream colleagues.

But the correspondence in the *North Star* did not only construct the world as a dangerous place where rampant despotism and upheavals threatened U.S. trade and business interests. It also challenged prejudices and, albeit from within, the discourse of American mission. The 1848 correspondence from Haiti is illuminating, especially when contrasted with the 1859 letter from Barbados by the *New York Times* correspondent, cited in Chapter 5. The editor prefaced "Harold's" first letter by saying that he had high expectations that the correspondence might help dismantle American prejudice against a free black republic, especially since "the people of this country in general, and the colored people in particular, are quite ignorant in regard to the character and condition of this most interesting Republic."[55] In the tropical island, where the *Times* writer would have seen a voluptuous goddess for his eye to feast upon, "Harold" saw a triumphant free land:

It would be impossible for me to describe the rapture with which I beheld for the first time, this land, unpolluted by the foul stain of slavery, and upon which the insults and the cruelties of the tyrant had been washed out in the blood of himself and his children. . . . As the day drew to its close, the scene was truly a most beautiful one. In the midst of these promitories, clad in the bright verdure of this region of perpetual summer, appeared a vast pile of limestone, known by the name of the Platform, and which, viewed from a distance, assumes the appearance of an *enormous fortress.* From its mimic parapets—thanks to a passing shower—there floated, apparently, like *flaunting standards,* two gorgeous rainbows, throwing *triumphal arches* athwart the course of our little vessel. [italics added]

While also lyric in tone, "Harold's" description of his approach to the island fits a discourse of militant racial pride, rather than the colonizer's eroticizing gaze as in the *Times* piece—a definitely alternative construction of the Caribbean world. It seems likely from Douglass' introductory editorial that "Harold" was black; the same cannot be said about "R.S.D.," whose race was impossible to determine from the *North Star* content. Nevertheless, in one of his London letters, "R.S.D." constructed the terms of the European revolutions in a way that both reinforces and contradicts the discourse of American mission. He wrote that he feared the French revolution might alienate other Europeans because of the violence in the Paris uprisings; he then added that England could not use the United States as a model for the European democratic movement, so long as U.S. slavery existed. He concluded, however, that the abolitionists' efforts kept him "hoping yet to be able to point to America as a proof of the safe and beneficent workings of self-government, and as a model worthy of the imitation of the world."[56]

In this statement, the contradictions by foreign correspondents for the antebellum black press are most evident. The construction of the rest of the world as inferior to the United States, which holds a unique exemplary role in history, is not so much challenged as qualified. The discourse of American mission is intact, but America must do away with black oppression. As noted, discriminating women correspondents like Johnson and Fuller wrote very much within the same parameters.

Despite their prejudices and stereotypes about foreign cultures, women correspondents and the *North Star* writers constructed the "world" from within a modified discourse of mission. Further, they, perhaps more than their fellow foreign correspondents, were interested in the "world" in order to construct a better United States, rather than being interested in the "world" per se. These writers expressed doubts about American superiority as long as Americans did not end slavery and racism, free women from oppressive conventions, and come to the aid of the republican movement across the world. But as soon as the United States could measure up to its ideals, these correspondents' writings lead one to believe the United States could be the privileged nation in history, one that the world could and should try to measure up to.

NOTES

1. Julia Edwards, *Women of the World: The Great Foreign Correspondents* (Boston: Houghton Mifflin Co., 1988): 21.

2. Michael Emery, Edwin Emery, and Nancy Roberts, *The Press and America*, 9th ed. (Boston: Allyn and Bacon, 2000): 180–181.

3. Maurine Beasley and Sheila Gibbons, *Taking Their Place* (Washington, D.C.: American University Press, 1993): 8. For example, Cornelia Walter edited the Boston *Transcript*, her family's paper, from 1842 to 1847.

4. Beasley and Gibbons, p. 8–9. Also, Marion Marzolf, *Up from the Footnote: A History of Women Journalists* (New York: Hastings House, 1977): 10.

5. For the exclusion that engendered several forms of alternative journalism, see Lauren Kessler, *The Dissident Press: Alternative Journalism in American History* (Beverly Hills: Sage Publications, 1984): 8–20.

6. Beasley and Gibbons, p. 9.

7. Marzolf, pp. 16–17. The *National Era* in the 1850s had a strong literary reputation; Bayard Taylor also wrote for it; see Donna Born, "Sara Jane Clarke Lippincott (Grace Greenwood)," *Dictionary of Literary Biography, vol. 43: American Newspaper Journalists, 1690–1872* (Detroit: Gale Research, 1985): 303–309.

8. Born, p. 306–307.

9. The identity, and consequently the writings, of Nancy Johnson were difficult to establish. Emery, Emery, and Roberts, p. 181, and Marzolf, p. 19, make reference to a Nancy Johnson writing for the *Times* from Europe in 1857; Ishbel Ross, *Ladies of the Press* (New York: Harper & Brothers, 1936): 46–47, does the same, but adds that Johnson (1818–1892) dedicated her book, *The Myrtle Wreath*, to Henry J. Raymond, her editor. *The Myrtle*

Wreath, published by Scribner of New York in 1854, does indeed contain a dedication to Raymond, "cordial and generous friend"; however, the frontispiece says the book's author is Minnie Myrtle. Further, the book is listed in the Library of Congress as written by Anna Cummings Johnson, also 1818–1892. Another book listed under Anna C. Johnson's authorship (in its frontispiece) is an 1859 book of travel writing from Germany, *Peasant Life in Germany* (New York: Charles Scribner); in the frontispiece, Anna C. Johnson is credited for writing the *Myrtle Wreath*. Finally, between June 1857 and January 1858, the *New York Times* ran six letters of European correspondence signed with the initials "A.J." It seems virtually certain that Minnie Myrtle, Nancy Johnson, and Anna C. Johnson were the same person.

10. "Women on the Frontlines: Do They Have a Different Agenda?," *Media Report to Women*, winter 1997, pp. 4–7.

11. William W. Stowe, *Going Abroad: European Travel in Nineteenth-Century American Culture* (Princeton, N.J.: Princeton University Press, 1994): xi, 5.

12. Shirley Foster, *Across New Worlds: Nineteenth-Century Women Travellers and their Writings* (New York: Harvester Wheatsheaf, 1990): 24.

13. Mary S. Schriber, *Writing Home: American Women Abroad, 1830–1920* (Charlottesville: University Press of Virginia, 1997): 5–7, 34–37.

14. Schriber, p. 9.

15. Schriber, pp. 61, 85.

16. Born, p. 306.

17. Grace Greenwood, *Haps and Mishaps of a Tour in Europe* (Boston: Ticknor, Reed, and Fields, 1854): 1.

18. Greenwood, p. 6.

19. Greenwood, pp. 189, 191. For the importance of the concept of gaze in imperialist discourse, see David Spurr, *The Rhetoric of Empire* (Durham, N.C.: Duke University Press, 1993): 13 ff.

20. Greenwood, pp. 397–400.

21. Greenwood, pp. 435–437.

22. Johnson, p. 10; *New York Times*, June 29, 1857, p. 3.

23. *New York Times*, June 29, 1857, p. 3.

24. *New York Times*, July 7, 1857, p. 2 (the second letter Johnson wrote was published first).

25. *New York Times*, June 29, 1857, p. 3 and January 4, 1858, p. 2.

26. *New York Times*, July 13, 1857, p.3 and January 4, 1858, p. 2.

27. *New York Times*, July 8, 1857, p. 2.

28. *New York Times*, July 11, 1857, p. 2.

29. Joseph Deiss, *The Roman Years of Margaret Fuller* (New York: Thomas Y. Crowell, 1969): 92–93.

30. On "travel-as-politics," see Schriber, pp. 132–165. Also, Margaret Fuller, *"These Sad But Glorious Days"* (New Haven, Conn.: Yale University Press, 1991): 8.

31. Schriber, pp. 141–144. Also, Stowe, pp. 118–124.

32. Timothy Roberts, *The American Response to the European Revolutions of 1848*. Ph.D. dissertation, Oxford University, 1998: 260–276.

33. Fuller, pp. 19–35.

34. Fuller, pp. 39–49.

35. Fuller, pp. 155–161.

36. Fuller, pp. 238–254.

37. Fuller, pp. 295–302.

38. Fuller, pp. 316–320.

39. Carter R. Bryan, "Negro Journalism in America Before Emancipation," *Journalism Monographs* 12 (1969): 1.

40. Kessler, pp. 27–29.

41. Bryan, p. 1, and Kessler p. 27.

42. Kessler, p. 31; Frankie Hutton, *The Early Black Press in America, 1827 to 1860* (Westport, Conn.: Greenwood Press, 1993): 11.

43. Kessler, p. 32.

44. Kessler, p. 31.

45. I. Garland Penn, *The Afro-American Press and its Editors* (1891, reprinted New York: Arno Press, 1969): 68–69.

46. George P. Marks, III, ed., *The Black Press Views American Imperialism* (New York: Arno Press, 1971): vii.

47. Kessler, p. 32–33.

48. Hutton, pp. 26–34.

49. *North Star*, February 25, 1848, p. 2.

50. *North Star*, March 24, 1848, p. 2.

51. *North Star*, March 31, 1848, p. 2.

52. *North Star*, April 21, 1848, p. 4.

53. *North Star*, June 23,1848, p. 3.

54. *North Star*, February 4, 1848, p. 3. William Lloyd Garrison was the foremost white abolitionist editor in the antebellum United States.

55. *North Star*, April 21, 1848, pp. 2, 4.

56. *North Star*, June 16, 1848, p. 3.

CHAPTER 7

THE EARLIEST AMERICAN FOREIGN CORRESPONDENCE: GIVING MEANINGS TO THE WORLD

> But there is a lot more to being an international news correspondent than joining an exclusive club or satisfying one's craving for adventure. You are being given the chance to cover history, to touch it, dissect it, look inside it and to see how the fate of nations comes to pass. . . . Your job is to provide context to distant events in a world made smaller by advances in technology.[1]

With these words, Louis Boccardi, president of The Associated Press, prefaced a handbook for AP foreign correspondents in 1998—almost exactly 150 years after the cooperative stationed its first correspondent abroad, Daniel Craig in Halifax, Nova Scotia. Boccardi's statement suggests that the purpose behind foreign correspondence has not changed greatly in a century and a half. Since the earliest American foreign correspondence was formally organized in the late 1830s, dissecting history and providing context for foreign events—giving meanings to the "world" for the American public—have constituted the purpose of the work of journalists abroad. Examining the earliest formally organized foreign correspondence in American newspapers, then, is crucial to an understanding of both the development of the profession and the evolution of the American commonsense understanding of other cultures.

American editors prized foreign news throughout the first half of the nineteenth century. The staple form of foreign news in U.S. newspapers before 1838 was the news digest, a summary of terse snippets of information, usually lacking background and context, reprinted from foreign newspapers. Digests continued to be printed in newspapers throughout the 1850s, when they became the exclusive domain of The Associated Press. But in 1838, a new form of foreign news appeared in U.S. newspapers—foreign correspondence, systematically prepared by (mostly American) reporters abroad. For the first time, American newspaper readers could see the "world" through the eyes of fellow Americans, sent there (according to their own writings) not only to gather the news but also to analyze the political and social culture of foreign countries.

The several meanings that these earliest American foreign correspondents gave to the "world" outside the United States likely helped construct and maintain a common sense about foreign cultures for American newspaper readers. Discourses found in editorials and foreign policy debates coincided generally with those found in foreign correspondence studied in this book. The most dominant was a discourse of American superiority, especially political, that was constructed repeatedly as the United States' providential mission to the rest of the world, either by "beneficial" intervention (on the American continent) or enlightening example (to Europe).

As the profession of foreign correspondent became more established, however, the correspondence appears to have become the site for discursive struggle between an ethnocentric understanding of foreign cultures and constructions reflecting attempts to understand the "world" on its own merits. Thus, while the early correspondence challenged the very common sense it simultaneously reinforced, it provided meanings that were not available in the other sources of foreign information, such as news digests, editorials, and foreign policy texts. Unexpectedly, ambivalent discourses appear in the writings of correspondents for the mainstream press rather than in the correspondence of a black newspaper or the women journalists studied. "Alternative" constructions were found in the "minority" correspondence, but they challenged the discourse of American superiority not so much on the basis of the writers' experiences abroad, but rather their experience of the United States as part of marginalized groups. Perhaps the greatest contribution of the earliest foreign correspondents lies in their focus at an unprecedented level on foreign cultures and in the admission by some, however ambivalently, that their own assumptions about the "world" contradicted the realities they encountered abroad.

The very fact that editors in the late 1830s for the first time sent reporters abroad fits the historical context of expanding newspapers and a new focus on news-gathering by reporters. It is likely that editors sent correspondents abroad—especially to Europe and Latin America—first of all to get the news, just like they increasingly sent journalists to Washington and other national centers of political or commercial activity. But since purely factual information continued to be provided by the news digests, the emergence of foreign correspondence may also signal the recognition that journalists abroad could see the world with different eyes and provide their readers with better information than could the reprinted digests.

It appears that American newspaper readers were keenly interested in foreign news, for it increased significantly throughout the antebellum period, more than quadrupling (in column inches) in two of the newspapers selected. Foreign news remained prevalent even as editors gave more importance to local news; in the 1859 *New York Herald* it occupied more than 60 percent of the news hole, more than in any other newspaper studied. Editors increasingly competed to be the first and the best with foreign news and, after the telegraph raised the level of competition, several editors (probably the most aggressive) put aside their differences to pool resources and start the first, and most enduring, news cooperative in the world, The Associated Press. This insured that all editors in the cooperative would get the same foreign news.

The digests were almost as dependent upon European newspapers as had been the American editors who had scrambled on boats to get packets of papers thrown from ships so they could publish news summaries from abroad. News digests conformed to a routine pattern of presentation and established a pattern of provenance and news prioritization that carried over into foreign correspondence. They focused predominantly on Europe, Mexico and Central America and on conflicts and sensational occurrences. While the sensational and the violent were also the fare of domestic and local news in the penny papers, the predominance of such news is particularly important when presented as a reality that most readers cannot validate with direct experience, as was the case with foreign cultures. The constructions in the digests depicted a dangerous and strange "world." The resulting image of the "world" was largely undifferentiated among countries or even along Western/non-Western lines; the real dichotomy was between the United States and the violent, odd, threatening non-American realm. By 1859, due to the dominance of The Associated Press in distributing foreign news nationwide, the digests had become very homogeneous, tersely written, and detailed in events but completely lacking any context or background that might suggest an opinion which could alienate some of the AP's members or clients.

Editors, however, apparently realized that the digests were not enough. Editors sought more than "a single electrician at a seaport town" could give them. According to what the correspondents wrote about their profession, a foreign correspondent was envisioned as a proven writer living in the center of the action and ready to report eyewitness accounts as well as to analyze foreign events. Editors probably wanted the context, background, and interpretation that reporters abroad could provide. Judging from what the correspondents wrote about their occupation and their editors' expectations, in the 1850s there was some understanding that the role of the (professional) foreign correspondent differed from that of the occasional travel writer; not surprisingly, then, the correspondents seemed concerned about some of the standards that were developing in journalism, such as accurate, eyewitness reporting. While correspondents also seemed to emphasize events and conflict in their foreign reporting, they understood their occupation as providing something the digests did not offer—analysis of foreign cultures.

The correspondents may have been influenced by the ways the "world" was constructed in editorials and in foreign policy debates. And the constructions in editorials and foreign policy texts likely colored the creation of meaning of foreign cultures for both the editors who edited foreign correspondence and the readers. Thus, the domestic context—the perceptions of the "world" in antebellum American culture—is necessary to understand both the discourses found in foreign correspondence and the influences on the creation of a common-sense understanding of foreign cultures.

The antebellum editorials dealing with foreign affairs reflected a discourse of Manifest Destiny, an ideology derived from the belief that the United States held a unique position, favored by Providence, as "leader and feeder of the civilized world," in Bennett's words. The discourse of American mission—American support could help the rest of the world to eventually rise to the American level—permeated editorials across political and sectional lines and remained a constant across the period studied.

Among several constructions that supported this discourse in the editorials read, one, especially in the *New York Herald* and the *New Orleans Picayune*, constructed the "world" as needing to reckon with the United States' superior power (an inherently contradictory construction that was also predominant among policymakers). Another construction portrayed foreign countries as naturally bountiful but inhabited by peoples so hopelessly barbaric and/or thoroughly misgoverned that there could be no hope of their rising to a par with the

United States if left on their own. Such a construction is a logical pre-cursor to a more overt imperialistic one, for it implied that intervention, as either annexation or influence, was not a selfish policy but rather the way the United States could fulfill its role in the world. The only qualifi-cation to this discourse seems to have been proximity: If Europe suc-cumbed to despotism, there was not much the United States could do; but the despots of Europe and Mexico could not be tolerated so close to the U.S. border, as in Texas or the Caribbean. In those cases of "next [door] neighbors," Americans had a right and a duty to "meddle," as the *New York Times* editor wrote in 1859.

In Washington, the discourse about the "world" revolved on the same principles of providential mission, but, interestingly, policymakers seem to have been significantly more fearful of foreign encroachment than either newspaper editors or foreign correspondents. Whether dis-cussing an action likely to cause war (like the annexation of Texas) or a technological advance hailed by its supporters as the herald of peace (like the Atlantic cable), congressmen debated the merits in light of the role of the United States in the international arena. Foreign issues were constructed as either favorable or detrimental to the establishment of the United States as a power worthy of the recognition and respect of the other main actors on the world stage, especially Great Britain.

Study of both editorials and foreign policy debates, then, shows that the "world" was constructed in relation to the United States through a discourse of mission that tended to ignore the idiosyncrasies of foreign cultures and implicitly diminish their intrinsic worth. In agreement with Schriber, who has written that "travel, whatever else it might be, was an American exercise in 'othering' for purposes of self-definition,"[2] findings suggest that constructing the "world," particularly within a discourse of American superiority, also constructs the meaning of the United States and of being American. However unconsciously done, such a discourse of foreign cultures represents the ultimate ethnocentrism. A student of late twentieth-century foreign correspon-dents has concluded that, in fact, most foreign news is actually national news.[3]

In this historical and discursive milieu, the importance of the devel-opment of foreign correspondence for the creation of an American commonsense understanding about the "world" cannot be underesti-mated. For the first time, after Bennett organized his corps of corre-spondents in 1838, American newspaper readers could see other parts of the world through the eyes of a fellow American who had gone abroad, and not merely as a traveler who sent home an occasional letter.

Rather, readers could receive news from someone who lived abroad precisely to report on a foreign culture.

The most significant finding in this book is that some of the earliest American foreign correspondents did challenge, however timidly, the discourse of ethnocentrism. That is, although foreign correspondence between 1838–1859 constructed the "world" within the discourse of American mission and superiority, some of it also contains the germ of a paradigm shift in its often contradictory constructions and some correspondents' admission that the "world" they saw did not always fit the discourse of American superiority. Rather, it encompassed realities that could be understood on their own.

The pervasiveness of the discourse of mission is borne out by foreign correspondence from different countries across the world. Comparison with the United States or with an American counterpart of any foreign subject is one of the earliest and most dominant constructions found in antebellum American foreign correspondence. Such attempts to make readers understand a foreign reality also bespeak ethnocentrism, especially since most comparisons sought to demonstrate the superiority of the United States. The varied comparisons, from similes used to familiarize the reader with foreign information to ideologically driven comparisons, elucidated little about foreign realities, but they likely reinforced American values and beliefs.

Some correspondents wrote condescendingly about foreign cultures, especially their political systems, and some resorted at times to ridicule in analyses and descriptions. Ridicule of foreign leaders was part of a construction also found in editorials—negatively stereotyping foreign leaders and the consequent argument that foreign countries could not be expected to better themselves on their own reinforced a sense of American political uniqueness. Some constructions held a whole native people to be incapable of self-government and of exploiting its country's natural resources, supporting an imperialistic trend. However, just as a Paris correspondent for the *New York Herald* sympathized with the efforts of the French colonial power to quell insurrection in North Africa, ignoring the right of the Algerians to their own country, a colleague corresponding for the *New York Tribune* from London attacked the idea that colonialism was meant to enlighten and benefit the conquered populations. In fact, only some of the *New York Herald* correspondents explicitly supported the doctrine of Manifest Destiny; some correspondents actually ridiculed the United States' quickness to resort to military means to restore what was perceived as an affront in international affairs.

Several correspondents for the *New York Tribune* and the *New York Times* criticized U.S. foreign policy and accused policymakers and U.S. diplomats of being woefully unprepared to deal with foreign questions, especially since they would not take the time to learn about the internal affairs of the countries they had to deal with. Even more significantly, some correspondence in the same papers reflected ambivalent constructions and it appears as a site for discursive struggle between the correspondents' cultural assumptions and their experiences abroad. Several correspondents questioned their own prejudices, and a few even recognized the stereotypes with which they approached foreign realities. The correspondents' sympathies with foreign countries, their culture, people, and struggles, are revealed in a discourse of the "world" that constructs foreign realities as not in line with the developing American common sense.

Two illustrative examples of this modified discourse, which was found in the later years, especially 1859, come from the *New York Tribune* and the *New York Times*. A *New York Tribune* correspondent from Italy, shaken by the devastation he observed in the areas just liberated from Austrian occupation, declared himself surprised by his observation that the Italian country folk, "generally very ignorant," were taking their hardships with a "philosophical equanimity" that he envied. (The correspondent seems conflicted between stereotypes he is not yet willing to modify, or perhaps even acknowledge, and a reality that contradicts them.) A *New York Times* correspondent from Barbados described the island within what Spurr has defined as eroticizing colonialist discourse,[4] as a goddess "voluptuously lying" there for his eyes to feast upon; and yet, when he started to directly experience life in Bridgetown, he wrote that he felt "rebuked" in his American prejudices against the black race. Walking through Bridgetown dispelled his prejudice that blacks could not live and behave in a civil manner. But the correspondent did not immediately discover and, therefore, question the discursive construction of the island in terms of submission and consumption. His correspondence, then, remained a site for two competing constructions of the "world," one culturally assigned and preceding the direct experience (e.g., the voluptuous goddess), the other based on the foreign country's own reality, at least as the correspondent saw it (e.g., the Barbadians' "Yankee" pride in their freedom).

The evidence of evolution in discursive constructions found in the writings of the 1850s correspondents for the *New York Tribune* and *Times* was not found in the correspondence where alternative discourses were expected—correspondence by women and in a black newspaper. The constructions of the "world" in the writings of Nancy Johnson and Margaret Fuller, as well as in the letters published in the *North Star*, did challenge the discourse of American mission, but only within its boundaries. Instead of constructing foreign cultures as other than a "world" that cannot measure up to the United States, they constructed the United States as needing to become better to be a better model. In fact, the writings of women correspondents and those in the *North Star* reveal an underlying ethnocentrism and seem to use foreign events as rebuttals to U.S. culture and the attitudes of Americans.

Thus, the focus of the discourse found in the writings by women and in a black newspaper was nearly exclusively on the United States, not on the "world." Johnson argued that the way American women were restricted to conventional roles was not a good example for Europe, but, on the contrary, might "demoralize" Europeans. "R.S.D." of the *North Star* wrote that only the work of abolitionists led to hope that America still might be "worthy of the imitation of the world." Thus, those correspondents seem to have been questioning American mission not because they found it irreconcilable with foreign realities, as did the two New York correspondents mentioned above, but because they found it irreconcilable with their own experiences as marginalized groups in the United States. In fact, Johnson and "R.S.D." "exploited" the American mission discourse to promote the causes of women's rights and black emancipation.

Fuller's experience in Italy led her, arguably, to an empathy with a foreign people hardly comparable to that of other correspondents. In her later correspondence, she identified with the revolutionary republican party so fully that she wrote of the Italian side in the war against the French as "our side." Nevertheless, she also ultimately constructed the Roman revolution of 1848–1849 within the discourse of American mission. Repeatedly in her dispatches, she appealed to Americans to support the Risorgimento, to become examples and lead (at least spiritually) the revolutionaries in their quest for freedom. She wrote that the Italians' cause "is OURS, above all others." In her eyes, a movement for national independence seems to have been fundamentally an American cause, for the United States was "the star of hope" and without it, the world would be left in a "bitter night."

The findings suggest, then, that the writings of Johnson, Fuller, and the *North Star* foreign correspondents did not construct an alternative discourse about the "world." Rather, their writing contained an alternative (and critical) discourse of the United States. The American political system needed to be more open to women, more just to blacks, more active toward overseas strugglers for freedom—and only then could the nation become true to its destiny as leader of civilization.

An alternative discourse, or at least a discursive struggle, began then not in the correspondence of writers outside the mainstream, but rather in the later correspondence of well-established newspapers like the *New York Times* and the *New York Tribune*. The correspondents' admission that their cultural assumptions might not fit foreign realities challenged the discourse of American superiority and provided a necessary impulse for the creation of new meanings.

The contradictory constructions in those mainstream newspapers carry two significant implications, especially since such contradictory constructions were not found in the virtually monolithic discourse in editorials and foreign policy debates. First, they suggest that the correspondents tried to achieve a deeper understanding of foreign cultures than that of editors in the home office. They seem to have understood their role overseas as eyewitness reporters of foreign affairs and as better informed analysts of foreign cultures and their meanings. A second implication relates to the lack of contradictory constructions in editorials or in congressional debates. The foreign correspondents may have felt freer than their own editors in constructing the "world" in ways not necessarily aligned with Washington foreign policies. A *New York Times* editorial in May 1859 argued that "beneficial intervention" in Mexico was necessary, because the country was incapable of self-government and its "turmoils" were so detrimental to U.S. citizens and their interests that Mexico could not be left "alone with safety." This contrasts sharply with a report from one of the same newspaper's Mexico correspondents, who sarcastically wrote in September 1859 that he was awaiting "some naval demonstration" to avenge the "insult to our national dignity" constituted by stolen mail—a veritable parody of interventionism. The contrast seems to suggest that the newspaper's editor did not hold his correspondents within obligatory discursive practices. The earliest American foreign correspondents thus apparently had both the ability and the opportunity to use their experiences abroad to defy prevalent constructions of the "world." While they did not create new meanings for foreign cultures, their challenging of mission-imbued constructions set the stage for a paradigm shift in the discourses about foreign cultures.

This study was, of course, limited by language and method. Discourse analysis relies on interpretation of the text both on the linguistic and cultural levels. The limitations of applying discourse analysis to history include the fact that linguistic nuances change over time and vary from person to person. The historian may understand words very differently from how nineteenth-century readers would have understood them.

Another limitation, inherent to a study of discourse and especially in history, is that one cannot determine the actual effect of a discourse on audience behavior or attitudes. The findings presented and discussed here might help us understand how foreign correspondents constructed the "world," but we cannot say whether the public accepted the newspapers' constructions, or whether any discourse had an impact on actions such as support or criticism of U.S. foreign policies. Nevertheless, given that the newspapers studied were widely read and that most of the readers likely had limited experience with the countries talked about in the correspondence, the earliest foreign correspondence probably helped shape Americans' commonsense views of foreign cultures. The strikingly modern resonance of some of the constructions, such as the dichotomous construction of political and social superiority and cultural inferiority to European countries, suggests the acceptance and endurance of some of the views of the "world" found in this study.

It must be stressed that there was no attempt to investigate how the discourses were created, or what might have influenced the texts and the construction of meaning between the time of the observed event in the foreign country and the time the news of it was printed in the United States. Certainly the correspondence was influenced by a series of variables, ranging from the idiosyncrasies of individual correspondents to their contacts in the foreign country, especially their sources (including, one might presume, interpreters) and editors in the home offices. Finally, if the number of newspapers studied makes it impossible to achieve broad generalizations, the findings are so consistent across newspapers of different political persuasions and editorial styles as to be highly suggestive about the discourses of the "world" in mid-nineteenth-century foreign correspondence.

Several questions arise from the findings and should be further investigated. Study of discourses about the "world" needs to be carried into the post-Civil War era. After 1866 and the completion of the Atlantic cable, competition with the telegraph for foreign facts (because of the fear that foreign correspondence would become "stale," as one correspondent expressed it) likely reached a new height and might have changed the prerogatives of postwar foreign correspondents. Also, in 1859, where this study leaves foreign correspondence, contradictions of the discourse of American mission were found. One wonders what happened to the discourses in foreign correspondence in the next thirty years, since, by the turn of the century, imperialism was established in U.S. foreign policy. The question of the influence of foreign correspondence on foreign policy, and vice versa, could also be studied in this context.

This book suggests that foreign correspondents seem to have had some liberty to construct the "world" differently from their editors and the political elite. Hardly a twentieth-century student of foreign correspondence, and perhaps hardly a journalist, has not complained about the lack of knowledge and understanding exhibited by the editors in the home office, especially when it comes to editing foreign copy. How was the relationship between editor and reporter (and foreign correspondent) constructed when the two professions began to be differentiated in the mid-nineteenth century? Does the homogeneity of newspaper texts increase or decrease proportionally with the growing professionalization of journalism and the differentiation of newsroom labor?

Yet another question raised by this study is how race and gender influence the construction of a journalistic text, especially when, as is the case in foreign correspondence, the topic is not directly related to either race or gender. As more blacks and women entered mainstream journalism in the later nineteenth century and early twentieth century, did their constructions of foreign cultures (or Washington affairs, for example) differ from those of white, male journalists?

Also, it would be interesting to know how the "world" was constructed by Washington correspondents who reported on foreign policy. Did they create different meanings of foreign cultures? Are there noticeable differences between their texts and those of their colleagues abroad? Is there historical support for one scholar's assertion that foreign correspondents tend to be more critical of U.S. foreign policies than is the Washington press corps?

And, finally, how have the discourses of the "world" evolved globally? How has the United States been constructed historically by foreign journalists? Did they perceive the discourse of American mission? How did they construct their own countries while abroad? Were there any similarities between their ways of creating meaning for the United States and those of American foreign correspondents constructing the "world?" Were correspondents from other countries also relying on comparison to understand foreign cultures? Did most or all foreign correspondents, while constructing the "world," also construct a meaning for their own country? Was ethnocentrism a characteristic of all foreign correspondence, or only of that for media in countries that dominated, or were going to dominate, the international stage (e.g., Great Britain)?

In conclusion, the construction of the "world" in the first two decades of formally organized American foreign correspondence evolved from that of dangerous, strange, misgoverned countries that needed to be enlightened by the light of American freedom in order to rise to U.S. levels, to cultures not entirely explainable within a discourse of American superiority and needing to be understood on their own terms. The later contradictory construction in foreign correspondence was likely a result of journalists' increased familiarity with foreign cultures. As their assumptions were challenged by their observations abroad, they came to challenge the commonsense values of the United States. Foreign correspondence increasingly sought meanings beyond the limits of American mission and questioned the very ideals supporting that discourse.

The earliest foreign correspondents were more factually accurate than the "electrician" and also better disposed, if their correspondence can be taken as evidence, to see the "world" as other than a collection of foreign peoples who cannot measure up to Americans. Reluctantly perhaps, some of the correspondents seem to have let foreign experiences challenge their perspectives of the "world" and of the United States.

These correspondents provided their readers with a unique opportunity for understanding the "other" (and the self) that they could not have had by reading the schematic news digests or the often jingoistic editorials. By that alone, they justified their presence abroad. As the AP's Boccardi instructed his international staff (the late twentieth-century successors of the "electrician at a seaboard town" and members of the world's largest news organization), foreign correspondence is about dissecting and giving meaning to the world's history in the making. The best argument for the existence of extensive foreign correspondence may have been validated by some of the earliest foreign correspondents in the history of American journalism. Twenty-first-century foreign correspondents may best fulfill their social responsibility as journalists if they complicate and challenge the American discourses about the "world" as did the first correspondents, whose pioneering work has been discussed here.

NOTES

1. Otto C. Doelling, ed. *Handbook for International Correspondents* (The Associated Press, 1998).

2. Mary Suzanne Schriber, *Writing Home* (Charlottesville: University Press of Virginia, 1997): 77.

3. Mark Pedelty, *War Stories* (New York: Routledge, 1995): 222.

4. David Spurr, *The Rhetoric of Empire* (Durham, N.C.: Duke University Press, 1993): 170–183.

BIBLIOGRAPHY

BOOKS

Baldasty, Gerald J. *The Commercialization of News in the Nineteenth Century.* Madison: University of Wisconsin Press, 1992.

Beasley, Maurine H., and Sheila J. Gibbons. *Taking Their Place: A Documentary History of Women and Journalism.* Washington, D.C.: American University Press, 1993.

Berger, Peter L., and Thomas Luckmann. *The Social Construction of Reality: A Treatise in the Sociology of Knowledge.* Garden City, N.Y.: Doubleday, 1966.

Beringer, Richard E. *Historical Analysis: Contemporary Approaches to Clio's Craft.* New York: John Wiley & Sons, 1978.

Berry, Nicholas O. *Foreign Policy and the Press: An Analysis of* The New York Times' *Coverage of U.S. Foreign Policy.* Westport, Conn.: Greenwood Press, 1990.

Blackett, R.J.M., ed. *Thomas Morris Chester, Black Civil War Correspondent: His Dispatches from the Virginia Front.* Baton Rouge: University of Louisiana Press, 1989.

Bleyer, Willard G. *Main Currents in the History of American Journalism.* Boston: Houghton Mifflin Company, 1927.

Blondheim, Menahem. *News Over the Wires: The Telegraph and the Flow of Public Information in America, 1844–1897.* Cambridge, Mass.: Harvard University Press, 1994.

Brown, Francis. *Raymond of the Times.* New York: W.W. Norton, 1951.

Burns, Richard D., ed. *Guide to American Foreign Relations Since 1700.* Santa Barbara, Calif.: ABC-CLIO, 1983.

Carey, James W. *Communication as Culture: Essays on Media and Society.* Boston: Unwin and Hyman, 1989.

Carlson, Oliver. *The Man Who Made News: James Gordon Bennett.* New York: Duell, Sloan and Pearce, 1942.

Chamberlin, Joseph E. *The Boston Transcript: A History of its First Hundred Years.* Boston: Houghton Mifflin Company, 1930.

Cohen, Bernard C. *The Press and Foreign Policy.* Princeton, N.J.: Princeton University Press, 1963.

Collins, Henry M. *From Pigeon Post to Wireless.* London: Hodder and Stoughton, 1925.

Cooper, Kent. *Barriers Down.* New York: Farrar & Rinehart, 1942.

Copeland, Fayette. *Kendall of the Picayune.* Norman: University of Oklahoma Press, 1943.

Crouthamel, James L. *Bennett's New York Herald and the Rise of the Popular Press.* Syracuse, N.Y.: Syracuse University Press, 1989.

Dabney, Thomas E. *One Hundred Great Years: The Story of the Times-Picayune from Its Founding to 1940.* Baton Rouge: Louisiana State University Press, 1944.

Davis, Elmer. *History of the New York Times, 1851–1921.* New York: New York Times, 1921.

Davison, W. Phillips, Donald R. Shanor, and Frederick T.C. Yu. *News from Abroad and the Foreign Policy Public.* New York: Foreign Policy Association, 1980.

Deconde, Alexander. *A History of American Foreign Policy.* 3rd ed. Vol. 1. New York: Charles Scribner's Sons, 1978.

Deiss, Joseph J. *The Roman Years of Margaret Fuller.* New York: Thomas Y. Crowell, 1969.

Desmond, Robert W. *The Press and World Affairs.* New York: D. Appleton-Century Co., 1937.

Desmond, Robert W. *Windows on the World: The Information Process in a Changing Society, 1900–1920.* Iowa City: University of Iowa Press, 1980.

Detti, Emma. *Margaret Fuller Ossoli e i suoi Corrispondenti.* Florence: Felice Le Monnier, 1942.

Dicken-Garcia, Hazel. *Journalistic Standards in Nineteenth-Century America.* Madison: University of Wisconsin Press, 1989.

Dorman, William A., and Mansour Farhang. *The U.S. Press and Iran: Foreign Policy and the Journalism of Deference.* Berkeley: University of California Press, 1987.

Durning, Russell E. *Margaret Fuller, Citizen of the World: An Intermediary Between European and American Literatures.* Heidelberg: Carl Winter, 1969.

Edwards, Julia. *Women of the World: The Great Foreign Correspondents.* Boston: Houghton Mifflin Co., 1988.

Emery, Michael. *On the Front Lines: Following America's Foreign Correspondents across the Twentieth Century.* Washington, D.C.: American University Press, 1995.

Emery, Michael, Edwin Emery, and Nancy Roberts. *The Press and America: An Interpretive History of the Mass Media.* 9th ed. Boston: Allyn and Bacon, 2000.

Fairclough, Norman. *Discourse and Social Change.* Cambridge, Mass.: Polity Press, 1992.

Fairclough, Norman. *Media Discourse.* New York: Edward Arnold, 1995.

Fenby, Jonathan. *The International News Services.* New York: Schocken Books, 1986.

Field, Henry M. *History of the Atlantic Telegraph.* New York: Charles Scribner, 1867.

Fortner, Robert S. *International Communication: History, Conflict and Control of the Global Metropolis.* Belmont, Calif.: Wadsworth Publishing Company, 1993.

Foster, Shirley. *Across New Worlds: Nineteenth-Century Women Travellers and Their Writings.* New York: Harvester Wheatsheaf, 1990.

Fuller, Margaret Ossoli. *At Home and Abroad.* Boston: Crosby, Nichols, and Co., 1856.

Fuller, Margaret. *"These Sad but Glorious Days": Dispatches from Europe, 1846–1850.* New Haven, Conn.: Yale University Press, 1991.

Fulton, Charles C. *Europe Viewed Through American Spectacles.* Philadelphia: J.B. Lippincott, 1874.

Furneaux, Rupert. *The First War Correspondent: William Howard Russell of the Times.* London: Cassell and Co., 1945.

Goldhagen, Daniel J. *Hitler's Willing Executioners.* New York: Alfred A. Knopf, 1996.

Graebner, Norman A. *Foundations of American Foreign Policy: A Realist Appraisal from Franklin to McKinley.* Wilmington, Del.: Scholarly Resources, 1985.

Gramling, Oliver. *AP: The Story of News.* Port Washington, N.Y.: Kennikat Press, 1940.

Greeley, Horace. *Glances at Europe: In a Series of Letters from Great Britain, France, Italy, Switzerland &c., during the Summer of 1851. Including Notices of the Great Exhibition, or World's Fair.* New York: Dewitt & Davenport, 1851.

Greenwood, Grace. *Haps and Mishaps of a Tour in Europe.* Boston: Ticknor, Reed, and Fields, 1854.

Hansen-Taylor, Marie, and Horace E. Scudder, eds. *Life and Letters of Bayard Taylor.* 2 Vols. Boston: Houghton, Mifflin and Co., 1855.

Harriman, Ed. *Hack: Home Truths About Foreign News.* London: Zed Books, 1987.

Heald, Morrell. *Transatlantic Vistas: American Journalists in Europe, 1900–1940.* Kent, Ohio: Kent State University Press, 1988.

Herman, Edward S., and Noam Chomsky. *Manufacturing Consent: The Political Economy of the Mass Media.* New York: Pantheon Books, 1988.

Hess, Stephen. *International News and Foreign Correspondents.* Washington, D.C.: Brookings Institution, 1996.

Hogan, Michael J., and Thomas G. Paterson, eds. *Explaining the History of American Foreign Relations.* Cambridge, Mass.: Cambridge University Press, 1991.

Hohenberg, John. *Foreign Correspondence: The Great Reporters and Their Times.* 2nd ed. Syracuse, N.Y.: Syracuse University Press, 1995.

Hudson, Frederic. *Journalism in the United States, from 1690 to 1872.* New York: Harper & Brothers, 1873.

Hunt, Michael H. *Ideology and U.S. Foreign Policy.* New Haven, Conn.: Yale University Press, 1987.

Hutton, Frankie. *The Early Black Press in America, 1827 to 1860.* Westport, Conn.: Greenwood Press, 1993.

Johnson, Anna C. *Peasant Life in Germany.* 2nd ed. New York: Charles Scribner, 1859.

Johnson, Anna C. (a.k.a. Minnie Myrtle). *The Myrtle Wreath, or Stray Leaves Recalled.* New York: Charles Scribner, 1854.

Kessler, Lauren. *The Dissident Press: Alternative Journalism in American History.* Beverly Hills: Sage Publications, 1984.

Kinsley, Philip. *The* Chicago Tribune: *Its First Hundred Years.* Vol. 1. New York: Alfred A. Knopf, 1943.

Kluger, Richard. *The Paper: The Life and Death of the New York* Herald Tribune. New York: Alfred A. Knopf, 1986.

Knightley, Phillip. *The First Casualty.* New York: Harcourt Brace Jovanovich, 1975.

Kruglak, Theodore E. *The Foreign Correspondents: A Study of the Men and Women Reporting for the American Information Media in Western Europe.* Geneva: Librarie E. Droz, 1955.

Lee, Alfred M. *The Daily Newspaper in America: The Evolution of a Social Instrument.* New York: Macmillan Company, 1937.

Lee, James M. *History of American Journalism.* New York: Garden City Publishing Co., 1923.

Linsky, Martin. *Impact: How the Press Affects Federal Policymaking.* New York: W.W. Norton, 1986.

MacKinnon, Stephen R., and Oris Friesen. *China Reporting: An Oral History of American Journalism in the 1930s and 1940s.* Berkeley: University of California Press, 1987.

MacNeil, Neil. *Without Fear or Favor.* New York: Harcourt, Brace and Co., 1940.

Marks, George P. III, ed. *The Black Press Views American Imperialism.* New York: Arno Press, 1971.

Marzolf, Marion. *Up from the Footnote: A History of Women Journalists.* New York: Hastings House, 1977.

Mathews, Joseph J. *George W. Smalley: Forty Years a Foreign Correspondent.* Chapel Hill: University of North Carolina Press, 1973.

May, Ernest R. *American Imperialism: A Speculative Essay.* New York: Atheneum, 1968.

Merk, Frederick. *Manifest Destiny and Mission in American History: A Reinterpretation.* New York: Alfred A. Knopf, 1963.

Merrill, John C., ed. *Global Journalism: Survey of International Communication.* 2nd ed. New York: Longman, 1991.

Miller, Douglas T. *Frederick Douglass and the Fight for Freedom.* New York: Facts on File Publications, 1988.

Mills, Sara. *Discourse.* New York: Routledge, 1997.

Milton, Joyce. *The Yellow Kids: Foreign Correspondents in the Heyday of Yellow Journalism.* New York: Harper & Row, 1989.

Mindich, David T.Z. *Just the Facts: How "Objectivity" Came to Define American Journalism.* New York: New York University Press, 1998.

Mott, Frank L. *American Journalism: A History of Newspapers in the United States Through 250 Years, 1690 to 1940.* New York: Macmillan Co., 1941.

Nazfiger, Ralph O. *International News and the Press.* New York: H.W. Wilson Company, 1940.

Norton, Mary B., David M. Katzman, Paul D. Escott, Howard P. Chudacoff, Thomas G. Paterson and William M. Tuttle, Jr. *A People and A Nation: A History of the United States.* Vol. 1. Boston: Houghton Mifflin Company, 1982.

Pedelty, Mark. *War Stories: The Culture of Foreign Correspondents.* New York: Routledge, 1995.

Penn, I. Garland. *The Afro-American Press and Its Editors.* Reprinted. New York: Arno Press, 1969.

Perkins, Dexter. *The Monroe Doctrine, 1826–1867.* Baltimore: Johns Hopkins Press, 1933.

Pletcher, David M. *The Diplomacy of Annexation: Texas, Oregon, and the Mexican War.* Columbia: University of Missouri Press, 1973.

Pollock, John Crothers. *The Politics of Crisis Reporting: Learning to be a Foreign Correspondent.* New York: Praeger, 1981.

Pratt, Julius W. *A History of United States Foreign Policy.* 3rd ed. Englewood Cliffs, N.J.: Prentice-Hall, 1972.

Pray, Isaac C. *Memoirs of James Gordon Bennett and His Times.* New York: Stringer & Townsend, 1855. Reprinted, Arno, 1970.

Pride, Armistead S., and Clint C. Wilson II. *A History of the Black Press.* Washington, D.C.: Howard University Press, 1997.

Reston, James. *The Artillery of the Press: Its Influence on American Foreign Policy.* New York: Harper & Row, 1967.

Rosenblum, Mort. *Coups and Earthquakes: Reporting the World for America.* New York: Harper & Row, 1979.

Rosewater, Victor. *History of Cooperative News-Gathering in the United States.* New York: D. Appleton and Company, 1930.

Ross, Ishbel. *Ladies of the Press: The Story of Women in Journalism by an Insider.* New York: Harper & Brothers, 1936.

Said, Edward W. *Covering Islam: How the Media and Experts Determine How We See the Rest of the World.* New York: Pantheon Books, 1981.

Schonberger, Howard B. *Transportation to the Seaboard: The "Communication Revolution" and American Foreign Policy, 1860–1900.* Westport, Conn.: Greenwood Publishing Corporation, 1971.

Schriber, Mary Suzanne. *Writing Home: American Women Abroad, 1830–1920.* Charlottesville: University Press of Virginia, 1997.

Schudson, Michael. *Discovering the News: A Social History of American Newspapers.* New York: Basic Books, Inc., 1978.

Schwarzlose, Richard A. *The American Wire Services: A Study of Their Development as a Social Institution.* New York: Arno Press, 1979.

Seitz, Don C. *The James Gordon Bennetts: Father and Son.* Indianapolis: Bobbs-Merrill Co., 1928.

Solomon, William S., and Robert W. McChesney, eds. *Ruthless Criticism: New Perspectives in U.S. Communication History.* Minneapolis: University of Minnesota Press, 1993.

Spurr, David. *The Rhetoric of Empire: Colonial Discourse in Journalism, Travel Writing, and Imperial Administration.* Durham, N.C.: Duke University Press, 1993.

Stevens, Kenneth R. *Border Diplomacy: The Caroline and McLeod Affairs in Anglo-American-Canadian Relations, 1837–1842.* Tuscaloosa: University of Alabama Press, 1989.

Stowe, William W. *Going Abroad: European Travel in Nineteenth-Century American Culture.* Princeton, N.J.: Princeton University Press, 1994.

Strout, Cushing. *The American Image of the Old World.* New York: Harper & Row, 1963.

Taylor, Bayard. *India, China and Japan.* New York: G.P. Putnam, 1855.

Thistlethwaite, Frank. *The Anglo-American Connection in the Early Nineteenth Century.* Philadelphia: University of Pennsylvania Press, 1959.

Thompson, Robert L. *Wiring a Continent: The History of the Telegraph Industry in the United States, 1832–1866.* Princeton, N.J.: Princeton University Press, 1947.

Tomlinson, John. *Cultural Imperialism: A Critical Introduction*. Baltimore: Johns Hopkins University Press, 1991.

Varg, Paul A. *United States Foreign Relations, 1820–1860*. East Lansing: Michigan State University Press, 1979.

Welter, Rush. *The Mind of America, 1820–1860*. New York: Columbia University Press, 1975.

Whitcomb, Roger S. *The American Approach to Foreign Affairs: An Uncertain Tradition*. Westport, Conn.: Praeger, 1998.

Williams, William A. *The Roots of the Modern American Empire: A Study of the Growth and Shaping of Social Consciousness in a Marketplace Society*. New York: Random House, 1969.

ARTICLES

Bjork, Ulf J. "Sketches of Life and Society: Horace Greeley's Vision for Foreign Correspondence," *American Journalism* 14:3–4 (summer-fall 1997): 359–375.

Born, Donna. "Sara Jane Clarke Lippincott (Grace Greenwood)," in *Dictionary of Literary Biography, vol. 43: American Newspaper Journalists, 1690–1872*. Perry Ashley, ed. Detroit: Gale Research, 1985, 303–309.

Brauer, Kinley J. "The United States and British Imperial Expansion, 1815–60," *Diplomatic History* 12:1 (1988): 19–37.

Brooker-Gross, Susan R. "Timeliness: Interpretation from a Sample of 19th Century Newspapers," *Journalism Quarterly* 58 (winter 1981): 594–598.

Bryan, Carter R. "Negro Journalism in America Before Emancipation," *Journalism Monographs* 12 (1969).

Cramer, Janet M. "Woman as Citizen: Race, Class, and the Discourse of Women's Citizenship, 1894–1909," *Journalism and Mass Communication Monographs* (1998).

Domke, David. "Journalists, Framing and Discourse About Race Relations," *Journalism and Mass Communication Monographs* 164 (December 1997): 1–55.

Domke, David. "The Press and 'Delusive Theories of Equality and Fraternity' in the Age of Emancipation," *Critical Studies in Mass Communication* 13 (1996): 228–250.

Gerbner, George, and George Marvanyi. "The Many Worlds of the World's Press," *Journal of Communication* 27:1 (1977): 52–66.

Giddings, T.H. "Rushing the Transatlantic News in the 1830s and 1840s," *The New York Historical Society Quarterly* 42:1 (January 1958): 47–59.

Gray, James L. "Bayard Taylor," in *Dictionary of Literary Biography, vol. 189: American Travel Writers, 1850–1915*. Donald Ross and James J. Schramer, eds. Detroit: Gale Research, 1998, 321–335.

Hall, Stuart. "The Rediscovery of 'Ideology': Return of the Oppressed in Media Studies," in *Culture, Society and the Media*. Michael Gurevitch, Tony Bennett, James Curran, and Janet Woollacott, eds. (London: Methuen, 1982): 56–90.

Kitch, Carolyn. "The American Woman Series: Gender and Class in the *Ladies' Home Journal*, 1897," *Journalism and Mass Communication Quarterly* 75:2 (summer 1998): 243–262.

Kress, Gunther. "Ideological Structures in Discourse," in *Handbook of Discourse Analysis: Discourse Analysis in Society* (vol. 4). Teun van Dijk, ed. London: Academic Press, 1985, Chap. 3.

Lent, John A. "Foreign News in American Media," *Journal of Communication* 27:1 (winter 1977): 46–51.

Ninkovich, Frank. "Interests and Discourse in Diplomatic History," *Diplomatic History* 13:2 (1989): 135–161.

Pallante, Martha I. "Horace Greeley," in *Dictionary of Literary Biography, vol. 189: American Travel Writers, 1850–1915*. Donald Ross and James J. Schramer, eds. Detroit: Gale Research, 1998, 132–137.

Pan, Zhongdang, and Gerald M. Kosicki. "Framing Analysis: An Approach to News Discourse," *Political Communication* 10 (1993): 55–75.

Schiller, Dan. "An Historical Approach to Objectivity and Professionalism in American News Reporting," *Journal of Communication* 29 (1979): 46–57.

Schramer, James, and Donald Ross, eds. "Introduction," *Dictionary of Literary Biography, vol. 183: American Travel Writers, 1776–1864*. Detroit: Gale Research, 1997.

Shaw, Donald L. "At the Crossroads: Change and Continuity in American Press News, 1820–1860," *Journalism History* 8:2 (1981): 38–50.

Struever, Nancy S. "Historical Discourse," in *Handbook of Discourse Analysis: Disciplines of Discourse* (vol.1). Teun van Dijk, ed. London: Academic Press, 1985, 249–271.

UNESCO. "News Values and Principles of Cross-cultural Communication," *Reports and Papers on Mass Communication* 85 (1979).

van Dijk, Teun A. "The Interdisciplinary Study of News as Discourse" in *A Handbook of Qualitative Methodologies for Mass Communication Research*. Klaus Bruhn Jensen and Nicholas W. Jankowski, eds. New York: Routledge, 1991, 108–120.

Vevier, Charles. "American Continentalism: An Idea of Expansion, 1845–1910," *American Historical Review* 65:2 (1960): 323–335.

Vevier, Charles. "The Collins Overland Line and American Continentalism," *Pacific Historical Review* 28:3 (1959): 237–253.

"Women on the Frontlines: Do They Have a Different Agenda?," *Media Report to Women* (winter 1997): 4–7.

UNPUBLISHED SOURCES

Doelling, Otto C., ed. *Handbook for International Correspondents* (The Associated Press, 1998).

Domke, David S. *The Press, Social Change, and Race Relations in the Late Nineteenth Century.* Ph.D. Dissertation, University of Minnesota, 1996.

Fibison, Michael D. *The Cold War Facade: A Comparison of U.S. State Department Policy Toward Romania and Text in Three Elite Newspapers.* M.A. Thesis, University of Minnesota, 1997.

Hall, Nora. *On Being an African-American Woman: Gender and Race in the Writings of Six Black Women Journalists, 1849–1936.* Ph.D. Dissertation, University of Minnesota, 1998.

May, Arthur J. *Contemporary American Opinion of the Mid-Century Revolutions in Central Europe.* Ph.D. Dissertation, University of Pennsylvania, 1927.

Roberts, Timothy M. *The American Response to the European Revolutions of 1848.* Ph.D. Dissertation, Oxford University, 1998.

Turk, Seyda. *Images of Foreign Nations: A Descriptive and Functional Analysis.* Ph.D. Dissertation, University of Washington, 1986.

INDEX

About the Author

GIOVANNA DELL'ORTO has experienced first-hand the intricacies of intercultural exchanges of meaning by working for The Associated Press in Rome, Italy, and along the U.S./Mexican border in Arizona. Fluent in four languages, she has traveled extensively across Western Europe and the Americas.